SERIES EDITOR: TONY HOLM

OSPREY COMBAT AIRCR

Me 262 BOMBER AND RECONNAISSANCE UNITS

ROBERT FORSYTH WITH EDDIE J CREEK

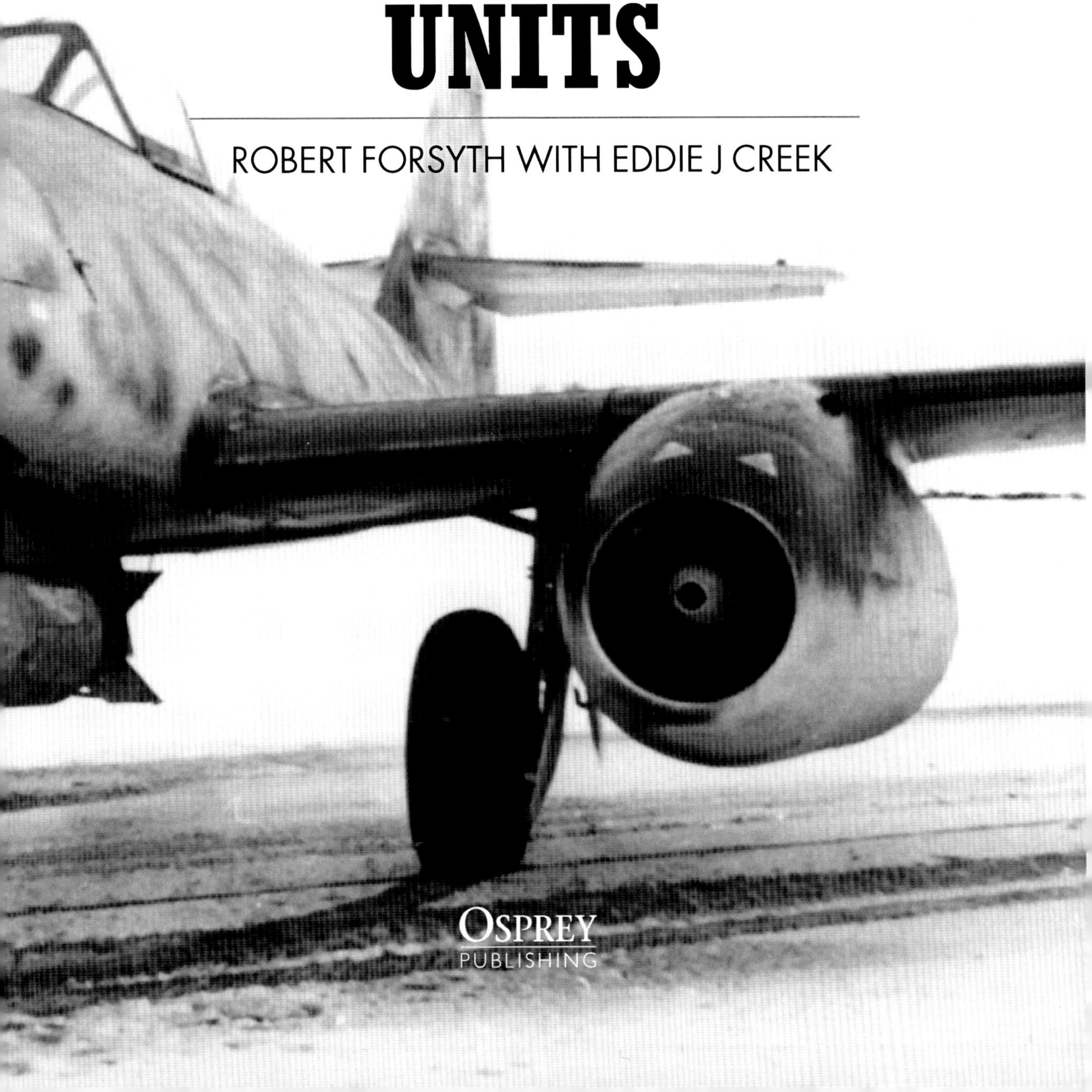

OSPREY
PUBLISHING

Front Cover
On 17 December 1944 – the day after German forces launched their *Wacht-am-Rhein* counter-offensive in the Ardennes – Me 262 jet bombers of I. and II./KG 51 conducted ground attack operations to the north of the core offensive area, targeting British troop and vehicle concentrations in northeastern Belgium.

Taking off in gloomy weather at 1000 hrs from II./KG 51's base at Hopsten, Hauptmann Rudolf Abrahamczik, *Staffelkapitän* of 2./KG 51, and Oberfeldwebel Hermann Wieczorek, also of 2. *Staffel*, were briefed to attack enemy motorised and armoured columns in and around Bree, a few kilometres west of the River Maas and close to the Dutch border. In a mission lasting 40 minutes, Abrahamczik's Leipheim-built Me 262A-1a Wk-Nr. 170106 '9K+LK' and Wieczorek's Schwäbisch Hall-built Me 262A-1a Wk-Nr. 110613 '9K+DK' were each loaded with a pair of SD 250 semi armour-piercing fragmentation bombs. Both aircraft had previously been used by KG(J) 54. Such harassment operations proved to be a painful thorn in the side of Allied ground formations as they advanced north and east towards the frontier with the Reich.

Mark Postlethwaite's specially commissioned cover painting depicts the moment that Wieczorek swept over the target in a customary shallow dive, dropping his bombs and pulling up, then using his superior speed to leave the scene before the enemy could react

First published in Great Britain in 2012 by Osprey Publishing,
PO Box 883, Oxford, OX1 9PL, UK
1385 Broadway, 5th Floor, New York, NY 10018, USA
Email: info@ospreypublishing.com

Osprey Publishing is part of Bloomsbury Publishing Plc

© 2012 Osprey Publishing Limited

All rights reserved. Apart from any fair dealing for the purpose of private study, research, criticism or review, as permitted under the Copyright, Design and Patents Act 1988, no part of this publication may be reproduced, stored in a retrieval system, or transmitted in any form or by any means, electronic, electrical, chemical, mechanical, optical, photocopying, recording or otherwise without prior written permission. All enquiries should be addressed to the publisher.

Transferred to digital print on demand 2017.

First published 2012
2nd impression 2013

Printed and bound by PrintOnDemand-Worldwide.com, Peterborough, UK.

A CIP catalogue record for this book is available from the British Library.

ISBN: 978 1 84908 749 0
eBook PDF ISBN: 978 1 84908 750 6
ePub ISBN: 978 1 78096 872 8

Edited by Tony Holmes
Page Design by Tony Truscott
Cover Artwork by Mark Postlethwaite
Aircraft Profiles by Jim Laurier
Index by Alan Thatcher
Originated by PDQ Digital Media Solutions, Bungay, UK

Acknowledgements
Many people have helped the authors over the years in researching Me 262 operations, but in terms of material for this book, our particular thanks are due to Nick Beale, Richard T Eger, Benjamin Evans, Martin Frauenheim, Brett Green, Manfred Griehl, Jan Horn, Jochen Mahncke, Tomás Poruba, J Richard Smith and Dave Wadman.

The Woodland Trust
Osprey Publishing are supporting the Woodland Trust, the UK's leading woodland conservation charity, by funding the dedication of trees.

www.ospreypublishing.com

OSPREY COMBAT AIRCRAFT • 83

Me 262 BOMBER AND RECONNAISSANCE UNITS

CONTENTS

CHAPTER ONE
'THAT ANSWERS THE *FÜHRER'S* QUESTION...' 6

CHAPTER TWO
***KOMMANDO SCHENCK* 13**

CHAPTER THREE
HITTING BACK 23

CHAPTER FOUR
HIGH-SPEED INTELLIGENCE 48

CHAPTER FIVE
***BODENPLATTE* TO THE BANKS OF THE RHINE 52**

CHAPTER SIX
TOO LITTLE, TOO LATE 76

APPENDICES 90
COLOUR PLATES COMMENTARY 91
BIBLIOGRAPHY 94
INDEX 95

CHAPTER ONE

'THAT ANSWERS THE *FÜHRER'S* QUESTION...'

By early 1943, the nature of the Luftwaffe's 'way of war' was such that its aircraft, deployed across three vast principal battlefronts, were expected, necessarily, to perform as multi-role combat machines. Indeed, the Luftwaffe had demonstrated impressive flexibility and resourcefulness in this regard. In the campaign against Britain in 1940 and the USSR in 1941-42, Bf 109E fighters had been adapted to operate as fighter-bombers, while He 111 bombers were pressed into service as emergency transports. In North Africa, Bf 109s and Fw 190s were used to conduct bombing trials, while from France, Bf 109Fs attacked shipping with bombs off the English coast. During the late 1930s, Ju 52/3m transports had flown as crudely adapted, but still effective, bombers during the Spanish Civil War. All of these adopted and adapted functions were quickly put into effect in the frontline.

In February 1943, Adolf Hitler ordered that *all* Luftwaffe fighters should be capable of carrying bombs so as to operate as fighter-bombers. Inherently, therefore, when a further *Führerbefehl* decreed that the much anticipated Messerschmitt Me 262 jet fighter should be built with the provision to carry 500 kg of bombs, there may have been a ripple of scepticism at the *Reichsluftministerium* and in the Messerschmitt design office, as well as at the various Luftwaffe test centres, but there was probably not much surprise. So it was that as early as 26 March 1943, Messerschmitt drew up plans for a fighter-bomber version of the Me 262.

Professor Willi Messerschmitt placed great hopes on his state-of-the-art fighter. The Me 262 had first taken to the air using pure jet propulsion on 18 July 1942 when company test pilot Fritz Wendel made a trouble-free flight from Leipheim. Following a delayed gestation, largely attributable to setbacks and problems with engine development and supply from BMW and Junkers, Wendel was able to report generally smooth handling during the maiden test flight, in which he achieved an unprecedented airspeed of 720 km/h.

Germany now possessed the technology it needed to respond to the ever-growing threat of Allied air power in the West. From then on, until mid-1944, development of the Me 262 forged ahead using a series of prototypes to assess all aspects of the aircraft. Initial testing was not without its problems, however. The Me 262 V3 crashed in August 1942 after three abortive attempts to take off, and on 18 April 1943 Oberfeldwebel Wilhelm Ostertag was killed when one of the Jumo 004 turbojets fitted to the Me 262 V2 flamed out, throwing the aircraft into a steep dive from which it never recovered.

Eventually, the Me 262 emerged as a twin-engined jet interceptor powered by two Jumo 004 turbojet units with single-stage turbines producing 8.8 kN of thrust at 8700 rpm. In the standard A-1a fighter configuration, it was planned to provide armament of four 30 mm MK 108 cannon mounted in the nose.

However, to satisfy Hitler's requirements, in the summer of 1943 Messerschmitt worked on a range of developments of the Me 262, extending the aircraft's fundamental role as an interceptor to that of fighter-bomber, high-speed bomber and reconnaissance aircraft. The concept of a high-speed bomber, or *Schnellbomber I*, proposed a design similar in shape to the standard Me 262A-1a fighter variant, but with an additional 2000 litres of fuel. This extra load was provided for by the incorporation of two 1000 kg thrust Jumo 004C engines with rocket-assisted take-off units. No defensive armament was to be carried, but alternative bomb loads of either a 1000 kg bomb, two 500 kg weapons, a pair of 250 kg bombs or one 700 kg BT 700 torpedo-bomb were proposed. Maximum speed at 6000 m was 785 km/h, with a range of 1180 km.

The *Schnellbomber Ia* saw cockpit and radio equipment moved forward to the nose and three more fuel tanks provided, containing an additional 2200 litres. Like the *Schnellbomber I*, the design was to be powered by Jumo 004C engines and have additional mainwheels with strengthened undercarriage legs. A similar bomb load to the *Schnellbomber I* was to be carried, but two MK 108s could be mounted in the nose. The *Schnellbomber II* had a new and much deeper fuselage and enlarged vertical tail surfaces, giving it a bulbous appearance. In this design, fuel supply was increased by 450- and 650-litre tanks in the nose and a 1300-litre tank behind the cockpit. Powered by Jumo 004Cs, the jet's bomb load was similar to that of the previous two designs, but the weapons were housed internally in the lower part of the forward fuselage. Maximum speed at 6000 m was 882 km/h, with a range of 1370 km.

A drawing produced by Messerschmitt AG at Augsburg from 22 July 1943 portraying the *Schnellbomber I* **proposal for a high-speed bomber version of the Me 262 interceptor. No defensive armament was to be carried, but a range of ordnance was proposed, including a torpedo-bomb**

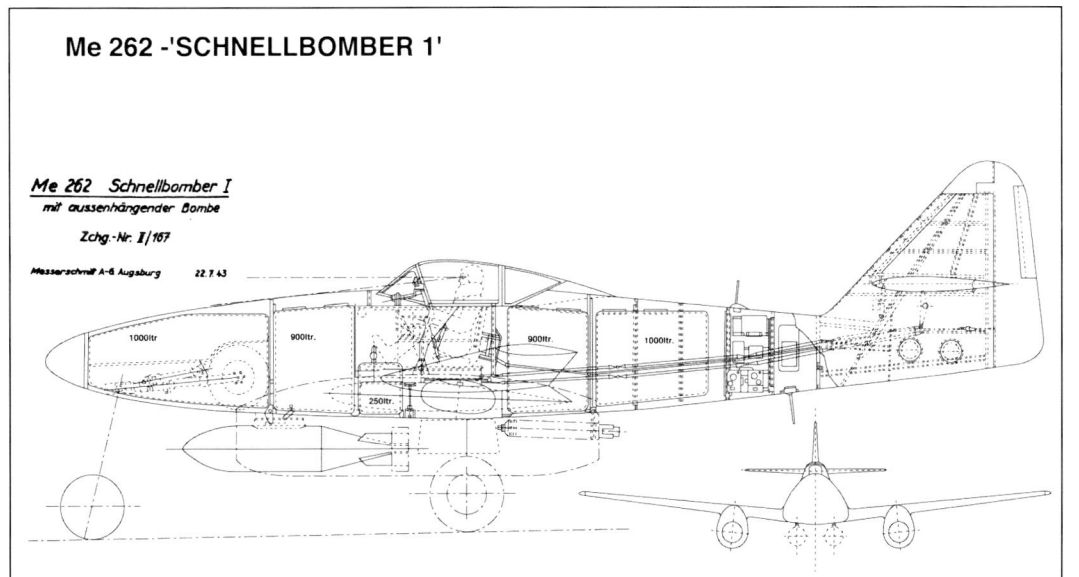

Me 262 -'SCHNELLBOMBER 1'

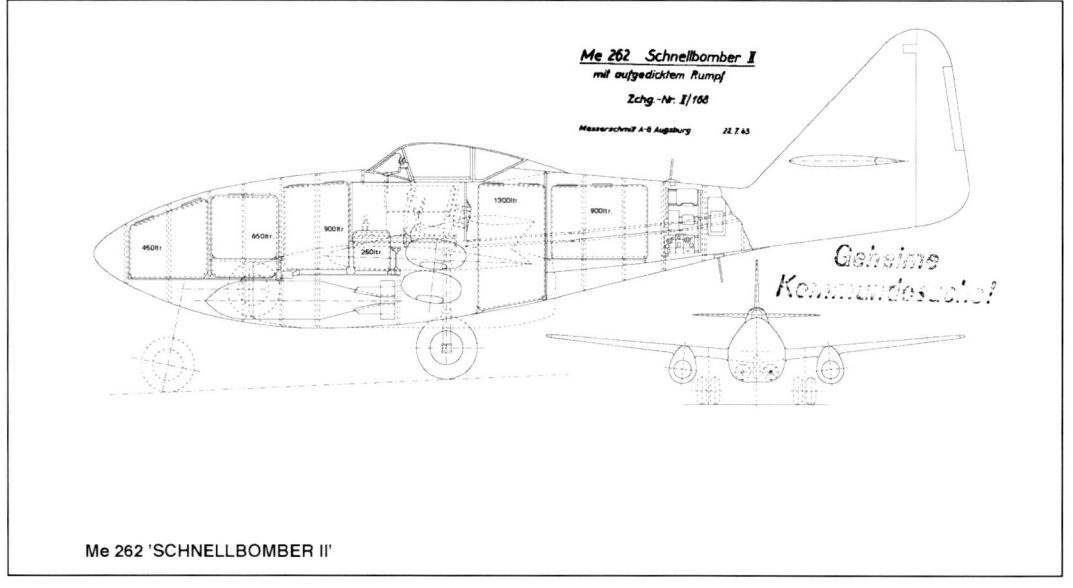

Me 262 'SCHNELLBOMBER II'

On 7 September 1943, Professor Messerschmitt attended the *Führer's* headquarters to brief Hitler on his latest aircraft designs. Ever the opportunist, Messerschmitt enthused about deploying the Me 262 as a high-speed bomber capable of attacking targets in England – a prospect which found great favour with Hitler. 'Its technical lead', Messerschmitt announced, 'is so great that this aircraft cannot come into service fast enough, otherwise we must expect the enemy to start coming over with similar aircraft before us, or simultaneously'.

Hitler agreed, and on 27 October he outlined his plan to combat the anticipated Allied invasion of France to the Commander-in-Chief of the Luftwaffe, *Reichsmarschall* Hermann Göring;

'The jet fighter with bombs will be vital, because at the given moment it will scream at top speed along the beaches and hurl its bombs into the massive build-up that is bound to be there.'

Just under a week later on 2 November, Göring, accompanied by *Generalfeldmarschall* Erhard Milch, the *Generalluftzeugmeister*, visited Messerschmitt's bomb-damaged manufacturing plant at Regensburg, where he met Willi Messerschmitt. It was at this meeting that this new, previously unforeseen dimension crept into the production programme of the Me 262 – the hand of the *Führer*, to which Göring was subservient. 'When the enemy attempts a landing in the West', announced Göring, 'and the first signs of confusion appear on the beach as tanks, guns and troops are unloaded and an immense traffic jam ensues, these fast machines, even if only a few of them, should be able to race through the heavy fighter screen, which the *Führer* expects in the event of such an attack, and drop bombs into this confusion'.

Göring demanded of Messerschmitt whether the Me 262 could carry bombs externally? 'Herr *Reichsmarschall*', Messerschmitt replied, 'It was intended from the beginning that the machine could be fitted with two bomb racks so that it could drop bombs, either one 500 kg or two 250 kg. But it can also carry one 1000 kg or two 500 kg bombs'. When Göring pressed the aircraft designer as to just how long it would take

A development of the *Schnellbomber* idea was the *Schnellbomber II*, which featured an improved fuel load housed in an expanded fuselage into which the bomb load was also housed

This photo, taken on 2 November 1943, shows Generalingenieur Roluf Lucht (second from left), senior engineer at the RLM, pointing to repair work carried out at the Messerschmitt works in Regensburg following the USAAF raid the previous August. *Reichsmarschall* Göring (second from right) and Professor Messerschmitt (far right) observe with grim expressions. It was during this visit that Göring impressed upon Messerschmitt Hitler's desire for a high-speed jet bomber with which to attack enemy forces in the event of the anticipated Allied landings on the coast of France

for a development aircraft to be so modified, Messerschmitt responded indifferently. 'Oh, not very long – two weeks, perhaps. It isn't really much of a problem, just a matter of fairing the [bomb] racks'. The *Reichsmarschall* beamed. 'That answers the *Führer's* question . . .'

Göring left with what he needed, and on 26 November he invited Hitler to Insterburg, in East Prussia, which was located conveniently near to the *Führer's* eastern HQ at Rastenburg. In an attempt to restore his declining prestige, he set up a display of some of the Luftwaffe's latest aircraft and weaponry. Examples of the Me 163 rocket interceptor were shown, as well as the Arado Ar 234 jet bomber. After a bungled commentary on the proceedings by Göring, the Me 262 V6 flew past. Hitler was impressed. He asked whether the aircraft was able to carry bombs. Messerschmitt, also in attendance, eagerly stepped forward and again reiterated that the jet could carry a bomb load of 1000 kg. The aircraft designer knew that work was already underway to adapt the jet fighter into a bomber, and

Whenever possible, aircraft designer Willi Messerschmitt (far right, pointing) ensured that he obtained approval from the very highest level for his aircraft designs. He is seen here in an illustration of this on 22 November 1937, when he unveiled to Adolf Hitler a mock-up of a large four-engined bomber project. Exactly six years later in November 1943, Messerschmitt would seek similar approval for the Me 262 jet fighter by telling Hitler that it would be able to carry bombs

9

he was keen to ensure that all surplus development projects were shelved in favour of the Me 262, in which he had placed so much of his faith.

That Hitler asked if the Me 262 was able to carry bombs may have been a misguided question from a man who had relatively little appreciation or knowledge of air strategy and aircraft design, as well as a philosophy founded primarily on offence, not defence, but, at the same time, it was perfectly understandable since every other Luftwaffe combat aircraft had already proved itself adequately capable of carrying bombs or performing in the fighter-bomber role. What was different about the Me 262?

The matter was not forgotten. On 5 December Hitler's Luftwaffe adjutant, Oberstleutnant Nicolaus von Below, cabled Göring;

'The *Führer* has called our attention again to the tremendous importance of the production of jet-propelled aircraft for employment as fighter-bombers. It is imperative that the Luftwaffe have a number of jet fighter-bombers ready for frontline commitment by the spring of 1944. Any difficulties occasioned by labour and raw material shortages will be resolved by the exploitation of Luftwaffe resources, until existing shortages can be made up. The *Führer* feels that a delay in our jet aircraft programme would be tantamount to irresponsible negligence. The *Führer* has directed that bi-monthly written reports, the first of which was due on 15 November 1943, be made to him concerning the progress of the Me 262 and the Ar 234.'

On 16 January 1944, Albert Speer, the Armaments Minister, and Milch were summoned to a conference with the *Führer* at which Hitler again emphasised that he was impatient to have as many Me 262s as could be made in the shortest possible time. Speer recorded that, 'During this conference Hitler showed that he planned to use this aircraft, which was to be a fighter, as a fast bomber. The air force specialists were dismayed, but imagined that their sensible arguments would prevail. What happened was just the opposite. Hitler obstinately ordered all weapons on board removed so that the aircraft could carry a greater weight of bombs. Jet aircraft did not have to defend themselves, he maintained, since with their superior speed they could not be attacked by enemy fighters. Deeply distrustful of this new invention, he wanted it employed primarily for straight flight at great heights to spare its wings and engines, and wanted the engineers to gear it to a somewhat reduced speed to lessen the strain on the still untried system'.

In May 1944, Unteroffizier Kurt Flachs was killed when the Me 262 V7 crashed on its 31st flight. The first series production aircraft suffered problems from burst tyres, electrical and mechanical maladies and recurring engine flameouts. In June 1944 alone, the S7 crashed on the 1st following an engine fire, the Me 262 S1 suffered a damaged

An Me 262A-1a standard interceptor fitted with racks for bomb-dropping trials in late 1944. Leipheim-built Wk-Nr. 110813 is seen here loaded with two 500 kg SC 500 bombs. The cable from a generator cart is plugged into the aircraft to charge its battery. This machine was used for training purposes by III./EJG 2 in 1944, and in 1945 it is believed to have been assigned to JG 7

starboard wing on the 11th and the nose, wings and both engines of the S3 were damaged in a crash-landing at Lechfeld on the 16th.

On 23 May Hitler ordered Milch, Speer and *Hauptdienstleiter* Karl-Otto Saur, the bluntly spoken engineer who was head of the *Jägerstab* (the emergency committee of industry officials formed to regenerate Germany's bomb-shattered fighter production), to a conference at the *Berghof*. Milch read out a list of projected aircraft production figures. At mention of the Me 262 as a *fighter,* the *Führer* questioned, 'I thought the 262 was coming as a bomber?' Milch explained that the aircraft could not become an effective bomber without extensive modifications.

Hitler was aware that the Allied invasion was due any day, and realised that the aircraft on which he had pinned his hopes for defeating it would not be ready. 'I only want it to carry a 250 kg bomb! Who pays the slightest attention to my orders? I gave an unqualified directive that the aircraft is to be built as a bomber'. He then demanded figures on the weight of the aircraft's guns and armour plate.

Saur produced the figures – 500 kg per jet. 'There you are. You can take all the guns out. The aircraft is so fast it doesn't need guns'. Milch urged Hitler to think again, but was subjected to further outrage. This was too much for Milch. '*Mein Führer*, even the smallest child can see that this is a fighter, not a bomber!' Hitler simply turned his back on Milch. The next day, Göring confronted his Chief of Staff, *General der Flieger* Günther Korten, his deputy, Generalleutnant Karl Koller and the *General der Jagdflieger*, Generalleutnant Adolf Galland, with the situation. They all agreed glumly that modifying the aircraft into a bomber would cause major design problems. 'You gentlemen seem deaf', declared Göring, 'I have kept repeating the *Führer's* perfectly clear order again and again. He doesn't give a hoot for the Me 262 as a fighter. He just wants it as a bomber, a *Jagdbomber*'.

On 27 May Göring cabled his senior staff officers and advisors;

'The *Führer* has ordered that the Me 262 is to be operated purely as a high-speed bomber. There is to be no mention of it as a fighter until further notice.'

Göring reinforced his position two days later at a conference of aircraft manufacturers and senior Luftwaffe officers that was held to discuss the Me 262's future. The *Reichsmarschall's* first action was to transfer the jet's jurisdiction to the *General der Kampfflieger* (General of the Bomber Arm);

'To avoid a misleading designation, I suggest that we call the new aircraft a "super-speed" bomber rather than a "fighter-bomber". Accordingly, further development of this model will be entrusted to the *General der Kampfflieger*. The *Führer* will decide which of those experimental models equipped with armour will be developed further as fighter aircraft. It is not that the *Führer* wants the new model to be only a bomber – quite the contrary. He is well aware of its potential as a fighter. However, he does want all those presently in production to come out as super-speed bombers until further notice. It is his desire that we concentrate on the bomber question, and that problems of bomb-carrying capacity, bomb rack release design, bombsight development and bombardment tactics be given paramount consideration.'

Göring then went on to explain how a super-speed bomber might be used in combating the coming invasion;

'On the English coast, for example, to bombard the beach while the invasion force was going aboard the boats, and against previously landed equipment during the unloading operations. As I see it, our aircraft could fly along the beach dropping their bombs in the confusion below. This is the way in which the *Führer* envisages the employment of the new model, and this is the way it will be!'

When Messerschmitt, who was present, inadvertently referred to the Me 262 as a fighter he was immediately interrupted by Göring. 'Will you please stop using that word *fighter*! The orders of the *Führer* must remain inviolable!'

On 22 June, just over a fortnight following the Allied landings in Normandy, Saur informed a gathering of his officials;

'Two days ago, on the express order of the *Führer*, another detailed discussion with him was held on the subject of the Me 262. *Reichsmarschall* Göring, *Generalfeldmarschall* Milch, General Bodenschatz and Minister Speer took part, and I was also present. At this conference the *Führer* clearly outlined the situation. In its present form the Me 262 must be used in the first place as a very high-speed bomber only. It must be produced earlier and in larger numbers than present planning has allowed for. The *Führer* has authorised that support for the implementation of this plan be drawn from the entire arms industry.

'Once again at this conference, at the special request of Göring, I gave the *Führer* a detailed account of the final development of the Me 262. I made it clear that measures were dictated by the present military situation, and that although the Me 262 would be available in sufficient numbers as a bomber in the first instance, with the arrival of the Ar 234 as *the* jet bomber, the Me 262 would revert to a fighter. The *Führer* has no objections to the machine being quoted in the programme at 500 fighters and 500 bombers for the present.

'Gentlemen, if we had had the Me 262 to make raids on enemy targets beyond the range of our other aircraft, then, according to the statements of both the *Führer* and Göring, the situation on the Invasion coast would have looked different from what it does now.'

Indeed, the 'situation on the Invasion coast' was precarious. What Hitler vitally needed was a fleet of high-speed bombers that were able to evade Allied fighter aircraft and attack the consolidating enemy landing operations in France with impunity. His hopes lay in events about to take place on airfields in southern Germany.

According to Hauptdienstleiter Karl-Otto Saur, in June 1944 Hitler viewed the Arado Ar 234 as 'the' jet bomber, and thus a more likely contender for the role than the Me 262A-2a. Mounted on its distinctive, jettisonable takeoff dolly, the Ar 234 V5 prototype rolls down the concrete runway at Alt Lönnewitz in early April 1944

KOMMANDO SCHENCK

Before converting to the Me 262 in mid-1944, the crews of II./KG 51 had operated the Messerschmitt Me 410 as a fast bomber in operations against the British Isles as V./KG 2. Here, Oberleutnant Rudolf Abrahamczik (centre), *Staffelkapitän* of 4./KG 51, is seen in conversation with other officers at Vitry, in France, following his award of the Knight's Cross on 29 February 1944 shortly after the *Gruppe* had been redesignated. Abrahamczik would later regularly fly the Me 262 on operations

In mid-May 1944, the I. *Gruppe* of *Kampfgeschwader* 51 'Edelweiss', based in northwest France under the command of the former *Kapitän* of 1. *Staffel*, Major Heinz Unrau (who had taken over in February), received orders to withdraw to Germany and prepare to convert from operations with the Me 410 fast bomber to the Me 262 fighter-bomber. From December 1943 I./KG 51 had been engaged in a campaign of night raids against England, using the Me 410 in harassment attacks on London, Bristol and targets along the south coast. However, attrition had been high, with heavy losses incurred over London during April.

While the bulk of the *Gruppe* went to Lechfeld, in early June 1944 a detachment of ground staff, led by the *Staffelkapitän* of 3. *Staffel*, Oberleutnant Eberhard Winkel, journeyed from Memmingen to Leipheim to begin familiarisation with the Me 262. Here, 50 technical personnel underwent a course covering maintenance of the Me 262 airframe and Jumo 004 turbojet engine. Conditions at Leipheim were far from ideal, with five of six hangars having been either destroyed or badly damaged in Allied air attacks. This in turn meant that much work on the jets was conducted – at some risk – in the open.

The bomber version of the Me 262 had finally emerged as the A-2 which, in its standard form, was to be equipped with two ETC 503 A-1 bomb racks beneath the forward fuselage and a *Revi* 16D reflector sight primarily designed for use with the reduced armament of two nose-mounted 30 mm MK 108

Major Heinz Unrau, *Kommandeur* of I./KG 51 (right) talks with Oberleutnant Georg Csurisky, *Staffelkapitän* of 1. *Staffel* (far left), in late 1944. Listening are Heinz Knobloch, the meteorologist of I. *Gruppe* (second left) and Oberleutnant Ludwig Albersmeier, Operations Officer

Me 262A-2a '9K+(white)YH' of 1./KG 51 was finished in a typical camouflage pattern applied to aircraft operated by I. *Gruppe* in the summer and autumn of 1944. The jet has had its upper MK 108 cannon ports faired over in conformity with its variant, and two ETC 503 bomb racks have been fitted under the fuselage. The nose cone is painted in 1. *Staffel* white

The ETC 503 bomb rack as fitted to the centre underside fuselage section of an Me 262. The clasps to which bombs were fitted can be clearly seen, as can the ejection chutes for spent cartridges fired by the aircraft's powerful 30 mm MK 108 cannon

The interior of a crude, wooden example of an ETC 503 bomb rack, showing the connection for the electric bomb release

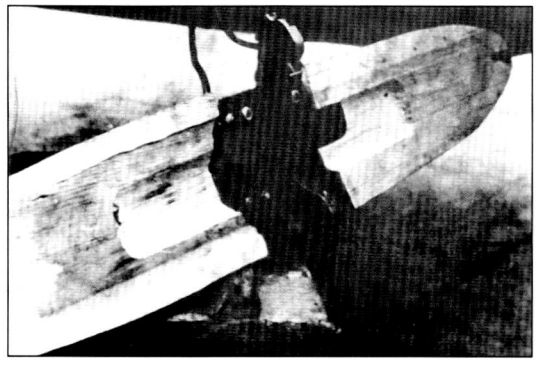

cannon. For bombing missions, the jet was to carry one 500 kg or two 250 kg bombs, or the equivalent weight in containers loaded with 10 kg anti-personnel bombs. Unlike in the Ju 88 (KG 51's most commonly used aircraft throughout the war), there was no downward-looking bombsight, but after some degree of training it was felt that pilots should become accustomed to using the *Revi* for bombing.

According to data furnished to *Luftflotte* 3 by technicians in Berlin in June 1944, the Me 262A-2a required a landing area 1500 m long and 400 m wide, with reinforced strips on either side. Permanent taxi tracks 12 m long were also needed, as was minimum obstacle clearance of 1:70 (and, if possible, 1:100) and a 'supplementary fuel installation' of 300 cubic metres, of which 100 cubic metres was to be near to the takeoff point.

To develop operational tactics for use by the Me 262 bomber, a special *Einsatzkommando* (operational detachment) was established from elements of 3./KG 51 under the leadership of Major Wolfgang Schenck, who had previously worked in the *Technische Amt* as an advisor to the *Generalluftzeugmeister*.

Schenck was a very experienced unit commander and tactician. He had returned from farming in East Africa to join the Luftwaffe in 1938 as a fighter pilot, being posted to II./JG 132. This *Gruppe* went through a series of redesignations, and by the time of the Polish campaign it had become I./ZG 1, with whom Schenck flew the Bf 110. Subsequently, he served in Poland and France, but was wounded in air combat and was hospitalised for three months. Upon his return to duties in September 1940, Schenck was assigned to the tactical evaluation unit *Erprobungsgruppe* 210, soon taking over command of 1. *Staffel*. Schenck conducted regular, and effective, fighter-bomber missions in the Bf 110 over southern England, targeting industrial areas and shipping – he accounted for 38,000 tons sunk.

Schenck later led I./ZG 1 in Russia, attacking enemy airfields and tanks and enjoying considerable success in his endeavours. He was awarded the Knight's Cross in August 1941, followed by the Oak Leaves in October 1942, before being withdrawn from operations to take up his position within the RLM. In late January 1943, Schenck returned to combat as *Kommodore* of ground-attack wing *Schlachtgeschwader* 2 in the Mediterranean. However, he was wounded in action and it was not until December 1943 that he returned to duties as *Inspizient der Schlachtflieger*, before being reassigned to the *Technisches Amt*.

Schenck would fly more than 400 combat missions in *Zerstörer*, ground-attack and bomber aircraft by war's end, accounting for some 40,000 tons of shipping sunk, 15 tanks destroyed and 18 enemy aircraft shot down. He would have a considerable influence on the development of bombing operations with the Me 262.

By 8 June 1944 – two days after the Allies had landed on the beaches of Normandy – the first pilots of 3./KG 51 had assembled at Lechfeld. No aircraft had yet been assigned to the *Geschwader*, however, so limited introductory training did not commence until the 30th, using the few Me 262s of Hauptmann Werner Thierfelder's *Erprobungskommando* 262 – the first operational jet test unit, which placed its emphasis on fighter deployment. From the 20th, Schenck's operational detachment (or *Einsatzkommando*) was christened *Kommando Schenck*, although it would be known during its existence by a variety of ad hoc names.

One of the first pilots of KG 51 to get airborne in the jet fighter at Lechfeld was Feldwebel Karl-Albrecht of 1. *Staffel* in 'Red 4' on the 24th, followed by his *Staffelkapitän*, Hauptmann Georg Csurusky, later that afternoon. On the 27th, the first jet assigned to KG 51 arrived at Lechfeld – an Me 262A-1a fighter! The following day, a second machine was delivered to I. *Gruppe*, which had previously been operated by the embryonic jet reconnaissance unit *Kommando Panther* (see Chapter 4). Indeed, the aircraft was flown in from Kitzingen by that unit's CO, Oberleutnant Herward Braunegg. In the early evening of 30 June, Feldwebel Karl-Albrecht Capitain flew the first mechanically ready Me 262A–2a bomber ('Black C') of the *Geschwader* from Lechfeld on an acceptance flight.

Training for the ground personnel of 3./KG 51 was completed in late June, whereupon they were moved to Lechfeld, coinciding with the arrival there of their counterparts from 1. *Staffel*.

Throughout June KG 51 had taken delivery of five Me 262A-1as, and by month end it had a total of

Maj Wolfgang 'Bombo' Schenck gives mission instructions to two of his pilots from the cockpit of an Fw 190 of SG 2 while serving on the Mediterranean Front in 1943. In June 1944, after fulfilling a subsequent staff appointment, this experienced tactician and holder of the Knight's Cross with Oakleaves was promoted to Oberstleutnant and assigned to establish *Kommando Schenck* in order to conduct operational trials with the Me 262 as a bomber on the Western Front

CHAPTER TWO

Feldwebel Karl-Albrecht Capitain of 1./KG 51 (right) was one of the early generation of pilots to fly the Me 262 as a jet-bomber at Lechfeld in June 1944. He is seen here with his *Staffel* comrades Feldwebel Helmut Bruhn (left) and Oberfeldwebel Erich Kaiser in the autumn of 1944

The only known photograph of the Me 262 V8 'VI+AC', which made its maiden flight in March 1944 and was the first example of the jet to be fitted with 30 mm MK 108 cannon. Sent to Lechfeld, the aircraft was used by *Erprobungskommando* 262 before being taken on by KG 51. Hauptmann Georg Csurusky and Leutnant Wilhelm Batel both flew it for familiarisation purposes in the summer of 1944. The jet was subsequently operated by 12.(Erg)/KG 51, before being used for testing purposes at Rechlin-Lärz

seven aircraft on strength, including at least one A-2a. The jets were coded 'Black A' through to 'G'.

On 6 July 1944 Saur addressed the *Jägerstab* to give details of Me 262 production plans;

'The aircraft is being produced as a *Blitz-Bomber*, its output last month being 22, then increasing to 60 in August, 150 in September, 225 in October, 325 in November and 500 in December. When output reaches 500 bombers, production above this level and up to 1000 will be switched to fighters. This programme for the Me 262, which should reach an output of 500 per month in the next few months, means that, although we have so far fallen far short of it, the programme until now in force for the type has been doubled. We are lagging badly behind in the fourth month's production of this type to date. Nevertheless, we have attempted not only to carry out the old programme, but we will also have to push through this doubled programme at all costs.'

Ten days later, on 16 July, Messerschmitt company minutes recorded various items of equipment needed for the Me 262A-2a. ETC 504 bomb racks, manufactured by *Mechanischen Werkstätten Neubrandenburg*, were to replace the Focke-Wulf designed ETC 503s, which had proven to be far from satisfactory when fitted to the jet, and rocket-assisted take-off (RATO) equipment was requested for 50 aircraft (the first to be delivered to KG 51).

After I./KG 51's tentative and unremarkable start at Lechfeld, on 7 July 1944 Leutnant Wilhelm Batel, the *Gruppe's* Technical Officer, accompanied by Unteroffizier Johannes Ebert, a radio operator from *Stab* I./KG 51, flew in an He 111 from Lechfeld to Leipheim to meet with Messerschmitt personnel to discuss the situation with regard to the pressing need for aircraft and parts. Meanwhile, the following day, the *Geschwaderstab* had established its headquarters at München-Riem, while more pilots arrived at Lechfeld around 10 July and spent the ensuing week test-flying the Me 262 and conducting bombing trials over the Ammersee, southwest of München. Simultaneously, another six jets were delivered to the *Gruppe* from Leipheim.

The first known loss to be suffered by I./KG 51 occurred on 14 July when the Me 262A-1a of Unteroffizier Walter Bentrott of 3. *Staffel*, assigned to *Kommando Schenck*, crashed in Lake Ammersee. The pilot was making a practice dive-bombing run at 30 degrees from 3000 m down to 1000 m at the time. His aircraft was seen to perform a series of violent manouevres as it emerged from clouds. Despite the Ammersee being a major landmark for navigation, it is probable that Bentrott struggled with the unfamilar speed of the Me 262 and flew the jet into the

One of *Kommando Schenck's* first aircraft was Me 262A-1a Wk-Nr. 130179 'Black F', seen here on a compass-swinging table at Lechfeld in July 1944

The nose section, cockpit, port wing and Jumo 004 of Me 262A-1a 'Black F' seen in profile at Lechfeld in July 1944. Note the two diagonal targeting lines painted on the canopy to assist the pilot in making a dive-bombing attack. This aircraft was fitted with a *Wikingerschiff* (Viking Ship) bomb rack mounted on the underside of the fuselage immediately aft of the nosewheel well, offset to starboard. This 'viking ship'-shaped rack could be fitted with an SC 500 bomb

Me 262A-1a 'Black F' was flown by pilots of *Kommando Schenck* and I./KG 51 for bombing trials during the summer of 1944. The aircraft had a red-tipped nose

water before he could recover from his dive.

The first, somewhat chaotic, move to the battlefront came on 17 July as Allied forces in Normandy fought their way across the Orne in their drive to take Caen, before preparing to launch the *Goodwood* offensive. The night prior to the move, Luftwaffe reconnaissance aircraft had used flare-lit photos to reveal the sheer weight of Allied traffic crossing the Orne bridges. On the evening of the 17th, Rommel's open-topped car was attacked by two RAF Spitfires as he was being driven from the front to his Army Group HQ. The German commander in Normandy was left unconscious with head injuries.

That same day some 150 ground personnel of 3./KG 51 were abruptly loaded onto lorries at Lechfeld and, after travelling for seven consecutive nights, arrived at Châteaudun, an airfield 110 km southwest of Paris and 175 km southeast of Caen. The *Geschwader* had once launched its Ju 88 missions against England from here. All other personnel of I./KG 51 (and Eberhard Winkel, the *Staffelkapitän* of 3. *Staffel*) remained at Lechfeld. At Châteaudun, the groundcrews were put to work immediately clearing rubble from the airfield and filling in bomb craters – tasks that they carried out until the middle of August.

Meanwhile, the remaining ground personnel from 3. *Staffel* under Winkel transferred to Memmingen, and 14 days later to Leipheim, for training on the maintenance procedures needed for the Me 262 and its new, advanced type of engines. Their move from Lechfeld meant that they avoided a bombing raid by the Eighth Air Force on the airfield on 19 July in which three Me 262s from I./KG 51 were destroyed – including 'Black F', one of *Kommando Schenck's* first aircraft, which caught fire due to exploding ammunition. This particular jet, which had been plagued by a number of mechanical problems including poor welding, wheel covers that did not fit, poorly installed fuel lines, loose undercarriage and ailerons and incorrectly balanced elevators, was no longer movable and was duly written off. Allied bombs destroyed or badly damaged another seven jets at Leipheim that same day.

On 20 July – the day Hitler's HQ at Rastenburg was rocked by Oberst Claus von Stauffenberg's bomb – the flying elements of I./KG 51, known as *Einsatzkommando*/KG 51, began their transfer to Châteaudun. The mission for the unit's nine aircraft was to bomb the enemy beachhead in Normandy and to attack and harass the Allied armies as they attempted to advance on Caen.

By this time each pilot from *Kommando Schenck* had made about four familiarisation and training flights in the Me 262. Messerschmitt's test pilot, Fritz Wendel, leading the company's *Technische Außendienst* (Technical Field Team), later reported on the situation facing the unit in the frontline;

'At the time when Major Schenck received his orders, operational employment [of the Me 262] as a fighter would have been possible – not so, however, as a bomber. There were many problems.

'The range was insufficient for bomber missions, since the operational base had to be located more than 100 km from the front due to strong enemy fighter activity over the front.

'For the increased takeoff weight with bombs, the undercarriage and tyres had to be strengthened.

'After the fitting of extra fuel tanks [into the Me 262], when dropping bombs in a shallow dive there were stability problems due to the centre of gravity [C of G] shifting towards the rear. To keep takeoff weight down, two of the nose guns had been eliminated. As a result, the C of G had moved further rearwards. Following flight tests, the rear tank was limited to 400 litres (instead of 600) to circumvent these problems, and rather complicated instructions on the method of drawing fuel from the rear tank issued. The 400-litre maximum was also introduced in order to keep the weight below 7000 kg.

'Since the tank had no fuel gauge and its fuel pump was prone to failure, the exact contents could not be checked before takeoff. Moreover, it happened frequently that there was still too much fuel in the tank after the bombs had been dropped, with resulting considerable stability problems – i.e. the aircraft pulled out from the dive on its own.

'There was no bombsight suitable for the single-seater. As a result the *Revi* fighter gunsight was used in shallow dive-bombing. This method had still to be tested and operational pilots instructed in its use.

'It was then found that the maximum speed of 850 km/h for aircraft fitted with fabric-covered control surfaces was being exceeded. Introduction

The Messerschmitt test pilot Fritz Wendel (right) visited I./KG 51 during the summer of 1944 on inspection visits, and he identified a range of operating problems with the Me 262 when deployed as a bomber. He is seen here in discussion with Major Heinz Unrau, *Kommandeur* of I./KG 51

of metal control surfaces had to be accelerated, tested and retro-fitted.

'The airframe had to be strengthened not only in order to permit speeds in excess of 850 km/h, but also for the fitting of both extra fuel tanks and takeoff rockets required for takeoffs with bomb loads.'

Also, during the afternoon of 20 July, 44 men transferred from Schwäbisch Hall to Lechfeld to join I./KG 51, but they came with no aircraft.

Meanwhile, Hitler had ordered that the Me 262 should not operate at altitudes of below 4000 m. However, the reality was that by late July 1944, German forces in the West were in full retreat, and conditions at Châteaudun were so chaotic that no operations were flown by *Kommando Schenck* before it transferred to Étampes on 12 August. On 26 July the unit reported an establishment of four pilots, with only two operationally ready, and five Me 262A-1s, of which four were serviceable.

On 21 July, during the sporadic training that continued at Lechfeld, Unteroffizier Herbert Winkler of 2./KG 51, like Walter Bentrott of a few days earlier, crashed into the Ammersee while on a twin-engined familiarisation flight in an Me 410 prior to converting to the Me 262. The list of fatalities continued into August when, on the 3rd, Leutnant Eduard Rottmann of 3./KG 51 crashed and was killed near the airfield at Lechfeld. Then, three days later, Feldwebel Willy Helber of 2. *Staffel* also crashed into the Ammersee while on a practice bombing flight.

On 2 August, Leutnant Walter Roth of 3. *Staffel* was ordered from France to Berlin to collect target maps from the RLM, and six days later no less a figure than Generalmajor Dietrich Peltz, the commander of IX. *Fliegerkorps*, visited I. *Gruppe* and impressed upon its personnel the importance of their forthcoming missions over the Invasion front. During the evening of the 9th, I./KG 51 received orders to commence operations. By this time the bulk of the *Gruppe* was still equipping and training at Lechfeld, with just *Kommando Schenck* in France. A total of 33 Me 262s had been assigned to the unit, of which 14 were ready for operations. A further 21 aircraft were planned to be assigned. The *Gruppe* also had a single remaining Me 410, but it was not operational. Meanwhile, *Stab*/KG 51 was at Landsberg with a single Me 410 and II. *Gruppe* was at Schwäbisch Hall.

Hitler was trying to push the Allies back to the sea. He had to prevent them from consolidating their hold in Normandy, but time was running out. *Generalfeldmarschall* von Kluge's Army Group B had failed in its critical drive on Mortain and Avranches, and the Allies were blasting shattered German divisions to pieces with their fighter-bombers, which operated with virtual impunity.

On 12 August, because of concerns about the pace of the Allied advance, ground personnel of 3./KG 51/*Kommando Schenck* left Châteaudun for Étampes, directly south of Paris. Just three days later they transferred again by road, this time to Creil, 45 km northwest of the French capital, ostensibly to be nearer to the planned zone of operations and to carry out similar preparatory work to the airfield there as they had done at Châteaudun. On their way to Creil, however, their

CHAPTER TWO

The clean, shark-like form of the Me 262 fuselage is displayed to good effect in this photograph of Me 262A-1a 'Black D' of *Kommando Schenck* at either Lechfeld or Châteaudun in the summer of 1944

Me 262A-1a 'Black D' of *Kommando Schenck* undergoes a landing gear test while mounted on tripod trestles at either Lechfeld or Châteaudun during the summer of 1944. In the event that power was lost in the portside Jumo turbo, hydraulic pressure would be lost, but the gear could still be lowered by means of a compressed air emergency system

One of KG 51's most regularly used forms of ordnance was the 470 kg AB 500 bomb container which could be loaded with either 37 x SD 10 fragmentation bombs or 116 x B 2 EZ incendiary bombs. Measuring 2362 x 500mm, one such container could be carried under the fuselage of an Me 262.

column was attacked by Allied aircraft. A handful of mechanics were killed and a number of lorries and spare parts destroyed. Finally, on the night of the 18/19 August, they relocated yet again to Juvincourt-et-Damary, 120 km to the east. On the evening of the 19th, *Luftflotte* 3 ordered that any remaining unused fuel, ammunition and supplies for the Me 262 were to be moved immediately from Creil to Coulommiers or Juvincourt as the ground situation dictated.

By 20 August I./KG 51 reported 36 Me 262s on hand at Lechfeld, of which 17 jets were operationally ready. Three Me 410s were also on strength, but none of these were operative. II. *Gruppe*, with 5. and 6. *Staffeln*, was at Schwäbisch Hall awaiting conversion to the jet, while the *Gruppenstab* remained at Landsberg. 4. *Staffel* was still due to commence conversion training to the Me 262. On the 24th, the *Einsatzkommando Schenck* reported that it had four operational pilots and four Me 262A-2as (three were serviceable). Oberfeldwebel Hieronymous Lauer of 3./KG 51 made a weather-monitoring flight that morning.

In what may have been the *Kommando's* combat debut, on the morning of 25 August four aircraft took off from Juvincourt to attack targets in the area of the bend in the Seine, northwest of Paris. All aircraft returned after midday. A second operation was flown in the mid-afternoon by the same four jets against the same target, but this time one made an emergency landing close to the front and was lost.

Between 0934-0942 hrs on 26 August, the remaining three jets took off to attack troop concentrations on the left bank of the Seine in the first of several sorties flown that day. Targets included enemy assemblies in woods near Chailly-en-Bierre (on which Lauer dropped two SC 500s) and on the road between Melun and Fontainebleau. The town of Melun was hit with two SC 500s, while targets nearby were struck with two AB (*Abwurfbehälter*) 500s fitted with SD 10s. At Mantes and in the area northeast of Bonnières-sur-Seine, the jets made a horizontal approach at 3000-4000 m, each one dropping an AB 500 container loaded with SD 10 fragmentation bombs into a wooded area southeast of Bonnières.

The next day, Lauer flew an Me 262A-1a, accompanied by one other jet, in the afternoon against Melun. Weather over Juvincourt hampered the operation, although the heavy fog and thick cloud did at least offer some protection from enemy fighters. Two SC 500s were dropped on Melun town centre, and a second operation against the Melun area saw a pair of AB 500s with SD 10s expended.

These initial missions met with little success, however, and according to Fritz Wendel the problem lay with the gunsights;

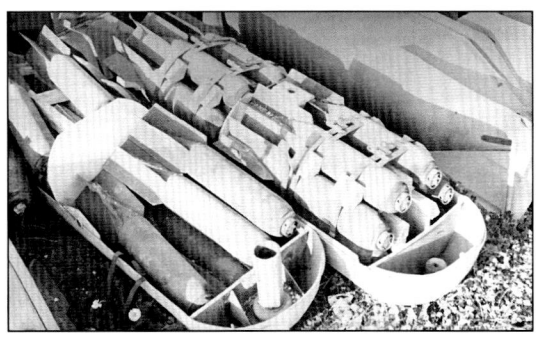

An AB 250 container loaded with 17 SD 10A fragmentation bombs. These weapons were dropped on troop assemblies, airfields and soft-skinned vehicles at low level

'In level flight, the *Revi* was useless for accurate bombing. Pinpoint targets could not be hit. *Kommando Schenck* was therefore unable to claim any tactical successes.'

Meanwhile, 27 August had also seen *Luftflotte* 3 issue orders to all of its units on airfields southwest of the line from Dunkirk to Charleville to move northeast, and to destroy their airfield facilities as they left. At 1700 hrs, IX. *Fliegerkorps* instructed *Einsatzkommando* I./KG 51 to prepare to move to Ath-Chièvres, southwest of Brussels, in Belgium. A total of 230 tons of J2 jet fuel was made available by the regional *Luftgau*, two tons of which had been delivered the previous day. At 1945 hrs, presumably overriding the earlier order to move to Ath-Chièvres, IX. *Fliegerkorps* instructed *Kommando Schenck* that it was to make preparations for an imminent transfer from Juvincourt to Volkel, in Holland, close to the German border, which was apparently specially equipped for Me 262s.

On 28 August, seven Me 262s attacked enemy troop assembly points using AB 500s loaded once again with SD 10 anti-personnel bombs. Following this operation, the threat of street fighting in the town of Juvincourt forced the *Kommando* to relocate to Ath-Chièvres. During the evening transfer flight, near Termond, Oberfeldwebel Lauer's jet was intercepted by two P-47s from the USAAF's 78th FG. Spotting Lauer below them, the American pilots went into a 45-degree dive, reaching 475 mph before they began to overtake the jet. Lauer began a series of evasive turns just as Maj Joseph Myers in the leading P-47 opened fire. The Me 262 crash-landed into a field near Haaltert, southwest of Aalst, before fire from the P-47's guns hit it. Lauer escaped injury, but his was the first Me 262 to be claimed by Allied fighters. Wendel's report, however, gave a different take on the incident;

'A total of nine aircraft have so far been employed operationally. Of these, one was badly damaged while still in France following an emergency landing near its base due to pilot disorientation and subsequent fuel shortage. The pilot was unhurt but the aircraft had to be blown up when the area was evacuated.

'Another aircraft had to make the transfer flight to Belgium with its undercarriage extended. The pilot [Lauer] had made an emergency landing on a French airfield due

Two Me 262s of *Einsatzkommando Schenck* take off from Juvincourt at dusk to attack Allied targets around the Seine in August 1944

to disorientation. During the final approach, the port engine stopped due to fuel shortage. The undercarriage had therefore to be lowered by compressed air. Since the wheel covers do not lock in the down position when compressed air is used, the undercarriage switch has to be set to "off" before the gear is retracted again. In this case the pilot neglected to do so (there are no instructions covering this at the moment) and, in consequence, the undercarriage could not be retracted.

'Due to its low speed with extended undercarriage, the aircraft was repeatedly attacked by several Spitfires [sic], coming under heavy fire. The two starter fuel tanks caught fire and the pilot made a forced landing on the main undercarriage with the nosewheel retracted. The pilot was unhurt. The badly damaged aircraft was later blown up.'

In the early evening of the 28th, of six aircraft slated to take off from Schwäbisch Hall for Juvincourt, only five did. However, one of the pilots who did get airborne failed to find Juvincourt and he was forced to make an emergency landing in his Me 262A-2a, incurring light damage, not far from the airfield.

Upon their arrival the jet bombers were placed under the tactical control of Peltz's IX. *Fliegerkorps*. According to one captured mechanic interrogated by the Allies, the first operations were flown from Juvincourt at this time at a rate of four to five sorties per day.

Meanwhile, the *Gruppenkommandeur*, Major Unrau, advised IX. *Fliegerkorps* that five more Me 262s and pilots should be available by 1 September. However, there was uncertainty as to whether it would be best to focus training on one *Staffel* or to bring the whole of I. *Gruppe* to a uniform state of conversion training.

The pilots of the *Einsatzkommando* (rated as the best in the unit) had received 'emergency training', but such training would not be suitable for most personnel, and therefore an adequate completion date was projected as 1 October.

For its part, IX. *Fliegerkorps* believed that, at that moment, any aircraft and pilots declared operationally ready should be sent immediately to Schenck's *Einsatzkommando* so that its testing of the Me 262 in frontline conditions would not be interrupted by shortages of men and machines. From then on, the *Korps* felt that the whole of I./KG 51 should be brought to a uniform state of readiness and deployed operationally.

Unrau also requested that a mobile field workshop be made available to the *Einsatzkommando* in France to enable efficient mobile operations in the zone of operations.

At 2100 hrs on 28 August, *Kommando Schenck* received its targets for the next day – the town of Coulommiers, east of Paris, and the area southwest of it as far as Rozoy. But the following day would also see *Kommando Schenck* make another move, this time further north to Holland, from where it would commence a new and more intense phase of operations.

Major Heinz Unrau, *Kommandeur* of I./KG 51, stands on the wing of an Me 262. In the foreground is, to left, Oberleutnant Georg Csurisky, *Staffelkapitän* of 1./KG 51 and, with his back to the camera, Hauptmann Rudolf Abrahamczik, *Kapitän* of 2./KG 51

HITTING BACK

As August gave way to September 1944, and the start of a wet, dismal autumn, the troops and armour of Field Marshal Montgomery's 21st Army Group broke out of northwest France and advanced steadily across Belgium to close on the port of Antwerp. By defending the Scheldt peninsula, Hitler wanted to force the Allies to rely on long lines of communication stretching as far back as Normandy, and to signal that there would be no easy push into Holland.

By 1 September, troops of the American Third Army had crossed the River Meuse, in eastern France, and were less than 100 km from Germany, while leading elements of the British XXX Corps had crossed the Somme and were heading towards Arras. The squadrons of the Allied tactical air forces were also leaving their airfields in Normandy to move ever eastwards. On 5 September, with the US First Army driving towards the German border, *Generalfeldmarschall* von Rundstedt, the Commander-in-Chief West, signalled his troops, 'Soldiers of the Western Front! I expect you to defend Germany's sacred soil to the very last!'

In the face of such Allied pressure, and after two days at Ath-Chièvres, the three pilots and operational aircraft of *Kommando Schenck* had arrived at Volkel, in Holland, by the morning of 31 August. This small contingent comprised Schenck, Leutnant Klaus Jäger and Oberfeldwebel Gerd Gittmann, the latter two pilots from 3. *Staffel*. The shot-down Oberfeldwebel Hieronymous Lauer and the wounded Feldwebel Horst Schulz of 3./KG 51 made their way to Volkel by alternative means.

At Volkel the jet pilots found an 1800 m runway sufficient for their needs, but much of the airfield had been destroyed by Allied bombing. Apart from a signals platoon, none of the unit's ground echelon had arrived, but gradually they turned up throughout the day, together with a quantity of spare jet engines. The *Kommando's* field kitchen had disappeared en route and five apparently overdue lorries also arrived, but they did not carry with them the anticipated equipment that was required by the unit. Schenck was also short of the 12 *Kettenkrad* semi-tracked towing vehicles that had been promised to his unit.

From his East Prussian HQ, Hitler ordered that every 20th jet built should be sent to the *Kommando* – the bulk of manufacture was now, necessarily, turned over to fighters. For a while, there was talk of a possible transfer to Eindhoven, the nearest practical alternative base.

Frustrating efforts still further, bad weather and a lack of readily available fuel prevented operations. Then, on 3 September, approximately 130 RAF Lancasters bombed Volkel, destroying two of the *Kommando's* Me 262s, including Schenck's aircraft. The British raid rendered the airfield unusable for operations and, the following night, in what British intelligence described intriguingly as a 'cloak-and-dagger move', the *Kommando*, with its one remaining aircraft, left for Rheine, near Osnabrück, the groundcrews crossing the Rhine near Wesel in darkness at 0200 hrs on the 4th.

CHAPTER THREE

Finished in a typical over-sprayed 'scribble' camouflage scheme used in the autumn of 1944, Me 262A-2a '9K+(white)YH' of 1./KG 51 also has a white nose cone and tail fin tip as *Staffel* identification markings. The individual aircraft code letter 'Y' is applied in an unusual curved style. This aircraft was fitted with under-fuselage ETC 503 bomb racks

On arrival at Rheine on 5 September, *Kommando Schenck*, and the experimental Ar 234 jet reconnaissance unit *Kommando Sperling*, did not receive the reception they expected when local *Wehrmacht* infantry attempted to disarm Luftwaffe personnel on orders of the *Reichsführer*-SS Heinrich Himmler, who decreed that any unit retreating from the west should be considered 'unreliable', and thus dealt with accordingly. Matters were swiftly, and 'efficiently', resolved by the Luftwaffe, however.

Simultaneously, in early September, Oberst Joachim Helbig, the *Kommodore* of LG 1, was made CO of *Gefechtsverband Helbig*, a new tactical air command formed from his *Geschwaderstab*, and briefed to support German ground operations along the Reich's frontiers with Belgium and Holland. Of paramount importance was the destruction of potential Allied crossing points over the Maas, the Waal and the Rhine, as well as the sustained harassment of enemy columns, troop assemblies and communications hubs. With an HQ at Köln, Helbig reported directly to *Luftflotte* 3, and was assigned elements of LG 1, whose Ju 88s had been operating over Normandy, NSG 2 (a night ground-attack unit equipped with Ju 87s), elements of KG 101 (which operated a small number of *Mistel* composites) and the Me 262s of *Kommando Schenck*.

To mid-September *Kommando Schenck's* operational area was mapped to a range of 250 km from its airfield (to Liège, for example). On 8 September, Leutnant Rolf Weidemann of 3./KG 51, in an Me 262A-2a, was lost to British flak northeast of Diest, in Belgium, while strafing troops with his MK 108 cannon from a height of 150 m. The remains of his aircraft were the first to be examined by Allied intelligence, its two damaged turbojets being subsequently sent to England for examination. Weidemann had collected his jet from Lechfeld just two days previously.

On 9 September the *Einsatzkommando* KG 51 had five Me 262s on strength. Following a weather reconnaissance flight by a jet to the Maastricht area, four Messerschmitts again attacked Diest, dropping four AB 500s loaded with SD 10s, but the pilots were unable to observe effects. Further attacks were not possible due to the deteriorating weather. The following morning, apparently reinforced by both personnel and aircraft, 15 Me 262s from *Kommando Schenck* attacked the road from Huy towards the west of Liège, the pilots observing hits on buildings southwest of the city and on the road from Liège to the west. On the 10th, Oberleutnant Werner Gärtner of 3. *Staffel* was reported missing after his Me 262 was hit by flak near Gomze, southwest of Verviers.

11 September 1944 saw ten Me 262s of the *Kommando* transfer temporarily to Schleswig, Wittmundhafen and Achmer airfields under the control of *Luftflotte Reich*, from where they mounted four attacks against Liège and enemy canal crossings near Beeringen. Explosions were observed around the canal. On the 12th the Me 262A-2a of Unteroffizier Herbert Schnauder of 3./KG 51 was hit as it overflew the viaduct over the Waal near Elden, 3.5 km southwest of Arnhem, while on a ferry flight from Volkel to Rheine. The pilot was killed in the ensuing crash.

Five of the seven Me 262s available to *Einsatzkommando Schenck* on the 13th made attacks in the Lommel area during the early morning, while the other two, including one jet flown by Oberfeldwebel Lauer, attacked troop concentrations north of Hechtel on the Maas and on the Scheldt Canal. Effects were not observed. Orders also reached the unit that, on instructions of the *Führer* himself, enemy troop assemblies were to be attacked in the Beverlo area. That day, Fritz Wendel reported on *Kommando Schenck's* operations thus far;

'At the time of writing [13 September], the *Kommando*, based on an airfield in northwest Germany, flies bombing missions. The field has three runways between 1400 m and 1800 m long. Operations are mounted as if flown according to a timetable. There have been hardly any problems with engines or airframes. The pilots are enthusiastic about the operations. They have often had to fly through formations of enemy fighters, but none of these have been able to get into a firing position. The *Kommando* has so far not tried to shoot down any enemy aircraft, but concentrated on completing its bombing missions.

'During my visit, attacks were flown repeatedly against Liège. The target was normally approached at 4000 m, the bombs being dropped in a steep dive. The distance from the air base to the target is 230 km. On return, also made at 4000 m, the aircraft's main fuel tanks still contained an average of 350 litres each. The normal flight time was exactly 50 minutes. According to the pilots, all bombs hit targets somewhere within the town. In one case a road was hit. I am not in a position to judge the military value of these operations.

'Two further losses occurred during my visit, the pilots failing to return from an attack on Liège. No news about the fate of the aircraft had been received before I departed. It can be assumed that the two pilots flew off in the wrong direction and came down behind the enemy lines.

'These losses were all due to faulty navigation – an opinion unanimously shared by the pilots. Apart from these losses, several emergency landings without damage had been made on other airfields for the same reason. The slow reaction of the compass and malfunctioning radio equipment, coupled with the unfamiliar high air speeds and short flight duration, are mainly to blame. After each shallow dive the compass rotates for several minutes. I believe that the compass is over-compensated, and therefore unreliable in its directional capacity. The FuG 16 ZY and FuG 25a only function properly during about five percent of all flights. It is therefore impossible to guide the aircraft by Y-Führung or Tornado-Peilung [radio navigation beams].'

In addition to these difficulties, Wendel also listed a host of minor problems, including two instances where the extra fuel tank transfer pump failed. Bomb release was therefore made with the C of G too far aft, and dive recovery was violent. In one instance this led to buckling of the wing skin over the engines. Subsequently, the jet concerned was modified. Furthermore, Wendel commented on problems associated with yawing – viewed as 'highly irritating' – at high speeds during bombing runs, although this was of relatively minor importance since precision attacks were not being made.

There were also problems with tyre damage, short circuits, nosewheel bearing seizures, the lack of a cockpit air vent (particularly when fuel was transferred wrongly, leading to overflow and an 'unbearable' smell in the cockpit that prompted nausea), aircraft arriving with the wrong camouflage scheme (a problem which was of particular concern to Major Schenck) and the inability to allow emergency bomb release.

In concluding his report, Wendel noted;

'Fifty missions were flown in three weeks of operations. The navigational problems, in addition to the well-known *Führerbefehl* forbidding attacks below 4000 m, make successful completion of missions entirely dependent on weather conditions. Sufficient J2 fuel has so far been available on all operational airfields.'

Two days later, as if to endorse his comments, planned attacks against troops near Neerpelt had to be broken off because of technical problems.

On 16 September the *Kommando* mounted attacks using five Me 262s against the breakthrough by XXX Corps near Beeringen, just east of the Albert Canal. Three jets dropped six bombs on Lommel, but the effects were not observed, while the other two had to break off their attacks and were forced to drop their bombs under emergency conditions.

The following day the Allies launched Operation *Market Garden*. In an unusually headstrong move, Field Marshal Montgomery had successfully persuaded Gen Eisenhower that under his control, the British Second Army, led by Gen Dempsey, could mount a 'rapid and violent' air-ground thrust across the Rhine and the Maas to form the spearhead of an advance into the German plain. The US 82nd and 101st Airborne Divisions would seize the Nijmegen and Eindhoven bridges, respectively, whilst the British 1st Airborne Division would take the bridge at Arnhem. Ultimately, bridgeheads would be established east of the Ijssel, while working with the US First Army to eventually isolate and surround the Ruhr. It was also hoped that the operation would affect the German ability to launch V2 rockets against London.

As a first move, in the early hours of the morning, a force of 200 Lancasters and 23 Mosquitoes from RAF Bomber Command struck at four Luftwaffe airfields near the Dutch-German border, including Rheine, where *Kommando Schenck's* runway was badly cratered. By late afternoon on the 17th, hundreds of Allied gliders had landed in the Netherlands, depositing 20,000 troops, 500 vehicles, 330 artillery pieces and hundreds of tons of equipment. Simultaneously, tanks and vehicles of XXX Corps advanced from Neerpelt along the Eindhoven road.

The facilities at Rheine were soon repaired, allowing three Me 262s of the *Einsatzkommando* to attack targets near Neerpelt on the 18th, during which one machine also flew a reconnaissance sortie over the front. Rheine was attacked again by Mosquitoes on 17/18 September.

Six pilots of 3./KG 51, including Hauptmann Hans-Christoph Buttmann, as well as I. *Gruppe's* Technical Officer, Leutnant Wilhelm

Batel, were ordered to transfer with Me 262s from Lechfeld to Rheine. Two jets arrived there safely, but three were unable to take off and one suffered tyre damage on landing at Rheine. On the 17th, Feldwebel Bernhard Bertelsbeck of 3./KG 51 crashed in an Me 262A-1a shortly after takeoff on a transfer flight from Leipheim to Lechfeld. The aircraft caught fire and Bertelsbeck was killed.

In the poor weather of 19 September, a pair of Me 262s of *Einsatzkommando* I./KG 51 flew reconnaissance flights in the Nijmegen-Arnhem area. The pilots spotted hundreds of gliders around Arnhem, and at 1600 hrs that afternoon 14 Me 262s were sent to attack them. Four jets struck in the Nijmegen-Groesbeek area, where elements of the 82nd Airborne Division were deployed, while the remaining ten went to hit the 1st Airborne Division around Deelen, Arnhem and Bennekom. Their bombs hit the targets, with a number of gliders observed to be on fire. In the afternoon, aircraft from I./KG 51 were detailed to bomb the railway bridge at Arnhem. Before the day was out, Hauptmann Winkel called Lechfeld from Rheine to report 'great success' against the gliders.

After troops from the 82nd Airborne Division had crossed the Waal on 20 September, followed by the tanks of XXX Corps, whose crews were near enough to see smoke rising from the fighting around Arnhem, *Kommando Schenck* mounted a concerted assault on the Nijmegen bridge and the nearby airfield, as well as troop and armour concentrations. On the 20th all operationally ready aircraft were deployed, with two jets also targeting British airbourne landings in the area north of Arnhem, but some bombs were jettisoned under emergency conditions.

Hauptmann Buttmann made a second attempt to fly from Lechfeld to Rheine, from where he was to sortie over Nijmegen and Arnhem, but en route he was forced down in a field. As he prepared for his descent, Buttmann realised that the area he had chosen was too constricted to allow the safe landing of his Me 262A-2a, so he quickly devised the idea of firing his twin 30 mm cannon, the recoil from which slowed him sufficiently so that he was able to touch down with minimal damage!

As with earlier operations, most of the attacks in the Allied drop and landing zones were made with aircraft fitted with single AB 500 containers holding SD 10 anti-personnel bombs, although on occasion aircraft would carry two SD 250 semi armour-piercing bombs. During these attacks, an Me 262 was damaged by a Spitfire IX of No 416 Sqn RCAF over Nijmegen on 28 September, and another by a Spitfire IX of No 441 Sqn RCAF east of the town on the 30th. At this time the *Kommando* reported an operational strength of 11 aircraft and 12 crews.

On 20 September, tactical control of *Kommando Schenck*, now more formally known as *Einsatzkommando* I./KG 51 (effectively 3. *Staffel*), was passed to the newly-formed *Gefechtsverband Hallensleben*, since Joachim Helbig had been wounded earlier in the month and replaced by Oberstleutnant Rudolf von Hallensleben. Formerly the *Kommodore* of KG 2, von Hallensleben had been given the new command following the disbandment of most of his previous unit. In a further reorganisation of the command structure, on 22 September *Luftflotte* 3 was redesignated *Luftwaffenkommando West*. At this time, II./KG 51 remained at Schwäbisch Hall, where it was still awaiting delivery of its 35 assigned aircraft. Pilot familiarisation was suffering as a result.

CHAPTER THREE

A member of the groundcrew prepares to tow out Me 262A-2a Wk-Nr. 170096 '9K+(white)BH' of 1./KG 51 from a line-up of the *Staffel's* jets on their concrete dispersal at Rheine using a ubiquitous semi-tracked *Kettenkrad* tractor during the early autumn of 1944. Note that the noses and gun ports of the aircraft in the line-up have been painted in the *Staffel* colour of white

Me 262A-2a Wk-Nr. 170096 '9K+(white)BH' of 1./KG 51 rolls past the camera while being towed by a *Kettenkrad* at Rheine in the early autumn of 1944. Such exposed, open-air manouevres would become increasingly difficult in late 1944 and into 1945 as the skies over German airfields on the Western Front became filled with hawking Allied '*Jabos*'

To the north, the fighting around Arnhem was entering its final phase – on 21 September, SS troops crossed the bridge and set up defensive positions to halt XXX Corps. Worse still, in mid-September, further to the east, the first American troops had penetrated the frontier of the Reich itself, having crossed the Sauer at Wollendorf, north of Trier. Two weeks later, elements of the American First Army breached what was thought to be the impenetrable Siegfried Line north of Aachen. The front was collapsing, and the Allies were now fighting within the borders of the Fatherland.

Throughout the gloomy autumn of 1944, KG 51 would struggle to provide badly needed air support to the German armies battling in the West. However, with its bases under continual attack from Allied fighters, against whom only the Me 262's speed was the saving grace, and with a shortage of fuel and bombs, this would prove challenging. The *Geschwader* had calculated that 65 tons of J2 fuel was needed to train just one pilot.

On 22 September, the *Einsatzkommando* I./KG 51 prepared all 11 of its Me 262s for strikes against troop concentrations in the Nijmegen area, but poor weather stalled the mission. Three days later, more bad weather forced a pilot conducting a lone armed weather reconnaissance to Nijmegen to drop his AB 500/SD 10, and upon returning to base he reported that there had also been 'defence' around the target.

On the 26th, the unit apparently having received reinforcements, 20 Me 262s were ordered to attack targets in the Nijmegen area during the afternoon and evening. Troop columns were attacked with nine AB 500/ SD 10 bomb combinations and 11 AB 500/SD 4s, but effects were not observed. Some of the jets encountered British fighters, and at 1830 hrs Flg Off Francis Campbell of the 2nd TAF's No 132 Sqn, flying a Spitfire IX, chased an Me 262 in the Nijmegen area and apparently inflicted damage on it. Nevertheless, the jet was able to outpace its assailant and Campbell was forced to break off his pursuit.

To the end of the month the *Einsatzkommando* I./KG 51 maintained a relatively high sortie rate. On the 27th the unit was issued orders by *Gefechtsverband Hallensleben* to strike at enemy assembly points in the area south of Nijmegen. Three Me 262s took off, but two jets were forced to break off early, and while the third dropped its bomb, the effects of the weapon could not be determined because of the poor weather. One machine was damaged on landing due to a collapsed nose wheel. On the 28th, Me 262s of I./KG 51 flew 34 sorties against

Nijmegen, although one aircraft did have to break off early because of undercarriage problems and it jettisoned its bombs. The area south of the town was struck with 33 AB 500/SD 10 ordnance combinations.

The presence of more 2nd TAF fighters again prevented further operations. Flt Lt J B McColl of No 416 Sqn RCAF inflicted light damage on an Me 262 over Nijmegen, but in a repeat of events on the 26th, the jet used its speed to escape the Spitfire IX. On the 30th, despite reports of enemy fighters near their airfield, three jets took off to strike the Nijmegen bridge carrying AB 500/SD 10s. The effects of the bombs on the bridge are not known. Later, an Me 262 was sent on a reconnaissance mission to Nijmegen, where the pilot could see that one section of the railway bridge lay in the water, but the road bridge was still intact.

Meanwhile, to the south on the 27th, during a transfer flight, Unteroffizier Wilhelm Erk of 2./KG 51 was lost near the village of St Ottilien, 16 km southeast of Lechfeld and close to the Ammersee.

Throughout September, KG 51 was assigned 46 Me 262As and two two-seat Me 262B-1s, but a lack of aircraft delayed II. *Gruppe* from starting conversion by one month – the whole of September. The need to maintain jets over the Nijmegen/Arnhem area would stop I. *Gruppe* from becoming operational in one location until the end of October.

The *Kommodore* of KG 51, Oberstleutnant Wolf-Dietrich Meister, arrived at Lechfeld on the 29th with *Major im Generalstab* Richard Schubert, a technical officer on the staff of *Reichsmarschall* Göring, on a fact-finding mission to ascertain why so few Me 262s were operational. Meister and Schubert subsequently took off in one of the unit's two-seat Me 262B-1as on a flight over the airfield. During takeoff, one of the RATO units fell away from the jet and hit the fuselage around the forward seat, which was occupied by Schubert. The impact damaged the hydraulics and the aircraft made a crash-landing.

From the end of September, I./KG 51 mounted reasonably consistent operations against the airfields at Chièvres, Eindhoven, Nijmegen, Volkel

A prime target for the jet bombers of I./KG 51 in the autumn of 1944 was the vital bridge over the Waal at Nijmegen. For some three weeks the *Gruppe* maintained an intensive campaign against the structure using fragmentation, high-explosive and armour-piercing bombs

In February 1945, following KG 51's attacks on the bridge at Nijmegen in September-October 1944, USAAF Intelligence produced a report on German jet-propelled aircraft in which this diagram was included to illustrate the Me 262's tactics during periods of daylight, darkness and at dusk

AT DUSK, when visibility was poor, and searchlights not yet operating, Me 262s come in at 1,000 feet and dive to 500 feet near bridge before releasing bombs.

DURING THE DAY, coming in at 25,000 feet, in a glide estimated at 15°, then diving to 18,000 feet.

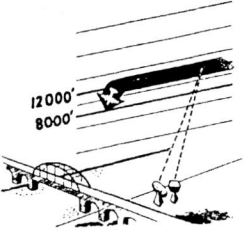

AT NIGHT, coming in at approximately 12,000 feet and diving to 8,000 feet. High speed and rapid change of altitude rendered radar, A/A predictors virtually useless.

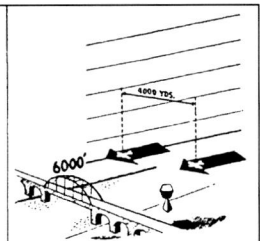

ATTACKS IN PAIRS, first Me 262 approximately 6,000 feet, second 4,000 yards behind and slightly below. Radar picks up first aircraft, misses second.

and Grave, using predominantly SD 250 *Sprengbomben* and AB 250 fragmentation containers.

By early October the *Einsatzkommando* must have received further aircraft, for on the 2nd, from 0630 hrs, no fewer than 35 Me 262s attacked various enemy troop assembly points around Nijmegen. Two of the jets were forced to break off, but the rest made it to the target area and released 11 AB 500/SD 10 combinations and 22 AB 500/SD 1s. One Me 262 was hit by flak and 17 others were interrupted in the process of their attacks by enemy fighters – probably Spitfires from 2nd TAF's Nos 122 and 125 Wings – but they still dropped their bombs.

KG 51 attacked Grave airfield on five occasions that day, the British suffering 35 casualties as a result of the jet raids, but there was no damage inflicted on Allied aircraft at the base, which remained fully operable. One Me 262 dropped an anti-personnel canister from about 10,000 ft which killed the No 125 Wing adjutant and one of the cooks in the Wing HQ. The HQ of No 127 (RCAF) Wing described the KG 51 attack;

'The airfield was bombed on five occasions, causing casualties, but only a small amount of damage, and this to tents and personal equipment only. It was apparent that the bombs were of the anti-personnel type and dropped from jet-propelled aircraft at 10,000 ft. The first attack was the only one that caused injuries to No 127 Wing personnel, and this was in all probability due to the fact that the bombs had landed and caused injuries before personnel realised what was happening. Three pilots were injured, two severely, and six other ranks and one officer received wounds of a minor degree. Immediately after this attack, personnel were warned of the action to be taken against these bombs, with the result that other attacks were abortive in so far as this Wing was concerned.

'The second attack came about noon, and bombs fell wide of the target on each occasion. Bombs fell on the No 125 Wing side of the landing strip on the third attack. Apparently No 125 Wing had not previously been warned, and its personnel were caught unawares. They had a number of severely wounded and moderately injured persons. In this attack, a number of Dutchmen living in the vicinity of the airfield also received serious injuries.

'The remaining two attacks were wide of the mark. After these attacks, personnel were seen starting to dig furiously, and slit trenches became a common sight. All personnel were ordered to wear their steel helmets at all times.'

The hazards of manning a flak battery during the jet attacks were illustrated by the uncomfortable experiences of one gun crew at Grave. The diarist of No 2819 Sqn, RAF Regiment, recorded;

'Quite a bit of action this morning. Enemy anti-personnel bombs dropped in the vicinity of the airfield. Jet-propulsion aeroplanes,

In the Public Archives of Canada this photograph is captioned as 'flak damage in Holland, 1944'. It was actually a fragmentation bomb dropped by a German hit-and-run raider (probably an Me 262) that caused the damage to this No 126 Wing Spitfire at Volkel, however. The 'all clear' following the raid has yet to be given, as both groundcrew are still wearing their tin helmets (*Public Archives of Canada PL 33414*)

Me 262s. Three gun detachment personnel slightly injured with flesh wounds in posterior.'

While taking off for a second mission from Rheine later that morning, Oberfeldwebel Lauer of 3./KG 51 suffered technical problems with the rudder of his Me 262A-2a that caused the aircraft to veer off the runway at speed and burst into flames when it crashed. Lauer suffered severe injuries, and he would spend four months in hospital and rehabilitation. His machine was one of two to suffer such a mishap that day at Rheine.

During the first week of October, *Kommando Schenck* continued to strike at Allied airfields and troop concentrations. These coincided with German ground forces launching attacks north of the Waal against XXX Corps. Southeast of Nijmegen, further attacks were made against the 82nd Airborne Division. However, with relatively few aircraft operationally ready at any one time, and no effective bombsights, *Kommando Schenck's* contribution to the German war effort was little more than derisory. An Allied report commented of the unit's efforts;

'They come in the dawn or just after, or at dusk and during the first few hours of darkness. Total number of bombs dropped has been small. There seems to be little coordination of effort, and aircraft come in singly or in groups of two or three. Anti-aircraft fire undoubtedly prevents accurate bombing. They drop bombs from considerable heights (about 10,000 ft), many of which are anti-personnel. During darkness HE bombing by Me 262s is more normal.'

On 3 October the *Kommando*, which had more or less been assimilated into 3./KG 51, reported a strength of ten aircraft and twelve crews. That day, all ten Me 262s were ordered to fly nuisance raids against Eindhoven, but two aircraft had to break off early. Two of the remaining jets attacked targets in the town, while six went for other targets. Ten SD 250s, two AB 500/SD 10s and an AB 500/SD 1 were expended, and no Allied defence was encountered.

The next day, in very bad weather, eight jets attacked Nijmegen airfield, one struck at Volkel airfield and three targeted Grave again. The Me 262s dropped two SC 250s, 18 SD 250s and two AB 500/SD 10s. On the way to, and from, the targets, Spitfires or Tempests were observed, but engagement was avoided. On the afternoon of 5 October, ten Me 262s flew nuisance operations from Rheine against Nijmegen and Chiévres, although one suffered engine failure shortly after takeoff and had to return. Seven jets dropped AB 250/SD 10s and SD 250s on the airfield at Nijmegen, while two expended AB 250/SD 10s on Grave.

Nijmegen bridge was also targeted on 5 October during the course of three operations involving ten aircraft. Nuisance attacks were made on Chiévres as well. Three jets from 3. *Staffel* were destroyed that day. Unteroffizier Gerhard Franke crashed in his Me 262A-2a at Engden, near Nordhorn, shortly after dropping his bombs near the Nijmegen bridge, while Feldwebel Joachim Fingerloos' machine turned over at Rheine following an emergency landing due to engine problems. Fingerloos was injured. Following an attack on the bridge, Hauptmann Hans-Christoph Buttmann was shot down in flames in the Nijmegen area by Spitfires of No 401 Sqn RCAF moments after releasing his 250 kg *Splitterbombe* and AB 250/SD 10. Ace Sqn Ldr Rod Smith, leading the Spitfire patrol, spotted a fast-moving aircraft. He recalled;

'I quickly recognised it as an Me 262. It kept on coming, and had obviously failed to spot us – probably because we were more or less between it and the sun, and it would, therefore, have to pass right through us. Just before it began to pass through us, it climbed to the left. I was fast pulling into position behind the Me 262 for a perfect shot, and I was already aiming along its path ahead of it. But that perfect shot was not to be. Another Spitfire, in a tight left turn like mine, suddenly appeared close in front of me, and almost in line between the Me 262 and me. If I fired I would risk hitting the other Spitfire, but for an instant I was tempted to fire a short burst anyway. I resisted.

'A second or two after he passed through us the Me 262 pilot rolled into a fairly steep dive, then half-rolled the other way to get himself upright and began banking and swerving from side to side. All the while he kept in the dive, crossing Nijmegen in a generally southwest direction. All of us dived down after him. "Tex" Davenport and I had to pull out at about 7000 ft because we were about to collide with each other, so I lost sight of the action for quite a few seconds. When I was able to look again I saw the jet had pulled out of its dive and was about 3000 ft over the southwest edge of Nijmegen, still heading southwest. It was no longer trailing smoke and was increasing its lead over several Spitfires, which were still chasing it but were then out of range.

'I thought the action was over, and that the Me 262 had got away, but quite suddenly it zoomed up into the most sustained vertical climb I had ever seen, leaving behind the Spitfires that had followed it all the way down. To my great surprise, and elation, its climb brought it up to where "Tex" and I were. As it soared up to us, still climbing almost vertically, the sweepback of its wings became very noticeable. Its speed, though still very considerable, was beginning to fall off, and with full power on I was able to pull up in an almost vertical position to within about 350 yards behind it – my maximum accurate shooting range.

'I aimed at one of its engine nacelles, and within two or three seconds a plume of fire began to stream from alongside one of them. The jet was then slowing down more than I was, and I was able to close the range to about 200 yards. I did not know that "Tex" Davenport was behind me, and was also firing!

'I finally closed in to 300 yards line astern and emptied the remainder of my guns – approximately 10 or 12 seconds – into the kite, observing strikes in the engines and fuselage. The aircraft was burning all this time. The pilot seemed to be unhurt, and put up a good fight during all of this. Halfway through our stall turns, when our noses had come down level with the horizon but our wings were almost vertical, I felt as if I were in a slow motion line abreast formation on the Me 262, to its right, directly below it. As the

A member of the groundcrew polishes the nose of an Me 262 of 1./KG 51. The nose and one gun port have been painted in the customary white of 1. *Staffel*. The small opening in the nose is the lens port for a BSK 16 gun camera

jet was only about 100 yards above me, I had a remarkable and unhurried look at it, side on. To my surprise I couldn't see the pilot's head, although the canopy was still fully closed. He must have had his head down for some reason.

'It began to dawn on me that when we had completed our stall turns we would be facing almost vertically downwards, with our positions reversed. The Me 262 would be close on my tail and I would be helpless. My nose went down and to the right. I had no control for quite a few seconds. After what seemed an age, during which I wondered if cannon shells would come smashing into me from behind, the Me 262 appeared a few yards away on my right. It was diving almost vertically downwards, as I was, but it was picking up speed more quickly and the plume of fire it was streaming had grown much bigger. It plunged on down and crashed within our lines just southwest of Nijmegen, sending up a billowing column of smoke.'

Some sources note that Buttmann attempted to bail out of the stricken jet, but that his parachute failed to open and he hit the ground and was killed between Overasselt and Nederasselt, 11 km from the bridge. He was the third officer, and fourth pilot, to be lost by the *Einsatzkommando* to enemy fighters.

From 6 October through to the 21st, Grave airfield, supporting operations by the First Canadian Army in its advance towards the Reichswald, became the main target for KG 51. However, on the 6th, seven Me 262s carried out nuisance attacks in the Nijmegen area with seven AB 500s loaded with SD 10s. Two more jets struck at the local airfield at Grave, each carrying a pair of SD 250s.

At daybreak on 7 October, 2nd TAF Typhoons attacked Rheine, but they inflicted little damage and there were no losses. Later that morning Hauptmann Georg Csurusky, *Staffelkapitän* of 1./KG 51, and Oberfeldwebel Erich Kaiser, also of 1. *Staffel*, took off from Lechfeld on a patrol. Southwest of Stuttgart, Csurusky observed a formation of Spitfires and attempted to attack them, but his MK 108 cannon jammed. He had approached to 200 m when he tried to open fire, so he simply flew through the enemy fighters at high speed and then climbed away. Evidently, this alarmed the Spitfire pilots sufficiently for them to disperse. That afternoon Csurusky was back in the air, and he managed to fire a short burst at a USAAF F-5 Lightning reconnaissance aircraft south of Würzburg, which then flew away.

To the north, seven Me 262s of 3. *Staffel* were deployed in three operations to the Nijmegen area and Grave airfield – seven AB 500s were dropped over Nijmegen and four over Grave. One jet was lightly damaged. In the target area enemy fighters were observed, and they briefly hindered the jets in their task.

In the early afternoon on the 7th, the *Einsatzkommando* received orders from *Gefechtsverband Hallensleben* that its attacks were to be restricted to airfield targets, with troop assembly points as a secondary target. But no further operations were subsequently flown until the 11th, when a solitary Me 262 bombed Volkel with two SD 250s, three jets attacked Grave with six SD 250s, three aircraft bombed Chiévres with three AB 500s loaded with SD 4s and four Me 262s attacked Nijmegen with four AB 500/SD 4s.

Flt Lt (later Sqn Ldr) R I A Smith joined No 412 Sqn RCAF in March 1944 after spending two months as a supernumerary at No 401 Sqn RCAF. Having claimed six kills flying Spitfires with No 126 Sqn during the defence of Malta in 1942, he added a further five as a flight commander with No 412 Sqn from 7 July to 27 September 1944. Given command of No 401 Sqn, Smith claimed two and one shared kills with this unit, including a quarter-share in the first Me 262 to be shot down by Allied fighter pilots on 5 October 1944. He ended the war with 13 and 1 shared destroyed, 1 shared probable and 1 damaged to his name (*DND PL 29398*)

CHAPTER THREE

Royal Engineers use a pump to drain water out of the crater left by the impact of Me 262A-1a Wk-Nr. 170093 '9K+BL', flown by Hauptmann Hans-Christoph Buttmann of 3./KG 51, following its crash between Overasselt and Nederasselt, 11 km southwest of the bridge at Nijmegen, on 5 October 1944. Buttmann fell victim to RCAF Spitfires from No 401 Sqn and came down in a landing area used by Allied gliders carrying airborne troops. In the foreground can be seen an RAF Intelligence officer examining the wreckage of what was the first jet to be shot down by Commonwealth air forces

Oberfeldwebel Erich Kaiser of 1./KG 51, in flying helmet and goggles, converses with groundcrew and the senior *Gruppe* engineering officer, Hermann Plattner (far right). In the background, out of focus, Major Heinz Unrau's senior mechanic observes from a *Kettenkrad*

The previous day, I./KG 51 had reported having 42 Me 262s on strength, of which 25 were serviceable. The *Gruppe* also had three Fw 190s available, of which two were serviceable.

Operations continued on 12 October, when seven jets again hit Volkel, dropping four SD 250s, Grave was attacked by three aircraft that dropped four SD 250s and one AB 500/SD 4 and Eindhoven was targeted by four Me 262s carrying four AB 500s and eight SD 250s. Another aircraft bombed targets at Helmond and Eindhoven. Two pilots broke off from these operations for reasons unknown.

Over the next four-and-a-half weeks, I./KG 51's lowest strength figure was four aircraft operationally ready out of eleven, while the high point came when the unit was able to muster 24 jets out of a total of 26. On 31 October, just 21 Me 262s out of 48 were available for operations.

On the 13th – the day the US First Army finally seized the hard won prize of Aachen (the first major German city to fall into Allied hands) – the *Gruppe* sent one Me 262 to attack Volkel, another to Chiévres and two to Eindhoven, each carrying two SD 250s. Unteroffizier Edmund Delatowski of 3. *Staffel* flew a mission to Grave, but he did not return. That day, Plt Off Bob Cole, flying a Tempest V of No 3 Sqn, encountered an Me 262 at 4300 m near Volkel. Cole fired at the jet as it passed 30 m above him. The Tempest became caught in the Me 262's slipstream, but Cole managed to give a straight and level chase for some 65 km. The German pilot then slowed his aircraft, possibly thinking he had thrown the British pilot off, at which point Cole fired a short burst at about 450 m from dead astern, which missed, before closing to 140 m and firing another short burst. According to a later RAF report;

'The Messerschmitt then appeared to explode like a flying bomb and threw off a number of pieces, including the pilot with his parachute. The aircraft went down in a spin and exploded on the ground, where the remains burnt out.'

Remarkably, Delatowski, who came down near Deventer, escaped with slight injuries.

The aircraft of Fahnenjunker-Feldwebel Edgar Junghans of 3./KG 51 was lightly damaged when one of its engines failed upon returning from a mission. The Me 262 was repaired at Rheine. At 2000 hrs that evening, *Einsatzkommando* I./KG 51 reported seven of its jets undergoing repair, with four operationally ready. On 14 October

34

the German unit attempted to take revenge against the RAF when three Me 262s bombed Volkel in a nuisance raid, dropping four SD 250s and an AB 500 loaded with SD 4s. On the 15th, two jets struck at Chiévres airfield with two SD 250s and two AB 250s loaded with SD 10s. Three aircraft also operated over Nijmegen on a nuisance mission, dropping six SD 250s.

Operations resumed on 18 October following two days of bad weather, when six Me 262s of 3./KG 51 flew an armed weather reconnaissance mission to the Nijmegen area. Four aircraft were forced to return to base early, probably due to the weather. Two jets reached the target, however, and dropped a pair of SD 250s.

On at least six days from 19 October to the end of month, a similar intensity of nuisance operations involving one or two jets – and at the most six – was maintained by 3./KG 51 against Allied airfields, troop assemblies and transport columns around Chiévres, Grave, Nijmegen, Eindhoven and Volkel. These missions, on the 19th, 20th, 21st, 24th, 28th and 29th, saw the customary ordnance of SD 250s, AB 500s and AB 250s loaded with SD 10s. On the 21st, Me 262s bombed Grave airfield, killing one airman and damaging 18 Spitfires from No 127 Wing, while two jets were claimed damaged by No 3 Sqn near Rheine. The unit also undertook weather reconnaissance missions along the Maas on the 25th and 28th, including one flown by the Technical Officer of I. *Gruppe*, Leutnant Wilhelm Batel.

At the end of October 1944, *Kommando Schenck* was officially re-incorporated into I./KG 51. By the end of the month it had received 25 Me 262s and had flown 163 missions involving 400 individual flights. Some pilots had flown up to six missions on a single day. Mission frequency would have been higher had it not been for the recurrence of bad weather over the target areas. The unit reported three jets as total losses due to combat and four lost to non-combat reasons.

Command of the *Geschwader* passed from Major Wolf-Dietrich Meister to Wolfgang Schenck on 21 October. The I. *Gruppe* command structure at the end of the month was as follows;

Kommandeur I./KG 51 – Major Heinz Unrau

1. *Staffel* – Hauptmann Georg Csurusky

2. *Staffel* – Hauptmann Rudolf Abrahamczik

3. *Staffel* – Hauptmann Eberhard Winkel as *Staffelkapitän* at Rheine, but with Major Wolfgang Schenck still nominally listed as the *Einsatzkommandoführer*, despite his appointment as *Kommodore*

Eight days after taking over control of KG 51, Schenck received a telephone call at his headquarters from Göring, who demanded to be given up-to-date information on the transmission of speed values for the Me 262. Schenck responded that maximum speed with a bomb(s) was found to be 700 km/h, and without ordnance it was a little under 800 km/h. In a climb, a top speed of 600 km/h could be attained. Göring apparently expressed some doubt as to the accuracy of these figures. This seems to have irked Schenck, who was moved to write a summary to the *General der Kampfflieger*, Oberst Walter Storp, on 29 October;

'I have the following explanations to the figures;

'1) The aircraft flown by the *Einsatzkommando* are the first of the series. Many complaints about the design exist.

CHAPTER THREE

Pilots of I./KG 51 listen attentively to their *Gruppenkommandeur*, Major Heinz Unrau, at Hopsten in the autumn of 1944. They are, from left to right, Oberfeldwebel Erich Kaiser of 1. *Staffel*, Oberleutnante Klein and Kühn (both signals officers), Oberleutnant Ludwig Albersmeyer (operations officer), Hauptmann Rudolf Abrahamczik (*Kapitän* of 2./KG 51) and Unrau

His head wrapped in bandages following his encounter with enemy fighters over Grave on 2 November 1944, Hauptmann Eberhard Winkel, *Kapitän* of 3./KG 51, relates his encounter to Major Heinz Unrau (far left) at Rheine

'2) A correct speed display requires a calibration in the airspeed indicator, which was not the case with these aircraft. Furthermore, the aircraft are only meant to reach their maximum speed after a considerable period (about 15 minutes). This condition could not be met during test flights because the flak range unit could only check when the aircraft were not too far away. Therefore, flying was undertaken with reduced power to start with.

'3) The speed figures from the test flights only refer to airspeed indicator readings.

'Figures known so far;

'1) Test flight with bombs at 3000 m and calculating the speed during a flight of 150 km – highest value = 670 km/h. The same aircraft without bombs over 250 km – highest value = 760 km/h.

'2) *Flugkapitän* Wendel's notes, referring to results from the test flights [state], "The figure of 670 km/h with bombs is about right if compared to my flights with the aircraft from the series. It is bad."

'3) Highest airspeed indicator figure reported by the *Geschwader* at 4000 m altitude without bombs = 830 km/h. As indication is higher than usual with this aircraft during landing, this could mean that above figures are incorrect.

'4) Average figure for top speed at 4000 m without bombs – below 800 km/h slowing to 750 km/h. Some pilots report even lower figures.'

By late October Montgomery's troops had reached the southern banks of the Scheldt, where their task was to flush the estuary of resistance so as to open Antwerp to Allied shipping.

On 2 November, Hauptmann Winkel flew his 40th combat mission in the Me 262. He was one of four pilots to take off from Rheine to strike at various airfields, including Grave, using AB 250/SD 10 combinations. As the jets flew over Grave, they encountered a formation of enemy fighters, probably Tempests of No 274 Sqn. Winkel positioned himself behind a British fighter and opened fire, but did not notice that another enemy machine had manoeuvred behind him and was firing its guns. Winkel received strikes to his cockpit, whereupon the canopy broke away. The Me 262's instrument panel also shattered and fell apart and Winkel suffered splinters in his head. Nevertheless, he somehow managed to fly the aircraft back to Rheine.

On the 5th, at Schwäbisch Hall, enemy fighters made a strafing attack and killed two ground personnel of II./KG 51.

Typical of the fight facing KG 51 at this time were the events of 7 November, when 16 Me 262s were ordered to operate against enemy targets from Rheine. Hauptmann Abrahamczik, Leutnant Oswald von Ritter-Rittershain, Oberfeldwebel Karl-Heinz Petersen and Leutnant Heinrich Haeffner, all of 2. *Staffel*, were instructed to fly a mission with 3. *Staffel* from Rheine. *Schwarmführer* Haeffner had to fly in a substitute machine since his usual aircraft was not functioning properly. At 1305 hrs the four pilots took off from Hopsten and flew through bad weather and poor visibility to Rheine, where they landed some 15 minutes later. However, because of the worsening conditions, the mission was scrubbed and the pilots were forced to abandon their jets at Rheine and travel by car to Hopsten. Upon their return it was discovered that Haeffner's Me 262 had been sabotaged, and the evidence pointed to dissident Italian workers.

Things took a turn for the worse the next day when the town of Rheine was subjected to a bombing attack by B-24s of the Eighth Air Force, during which the Operations Officer of I. *Gruppe*, Oberleutnant Rudolf Merlau, was fatally wounded at Waldhügel. The *Gruppe* Medical Officer, Stabsarzt Dr Paul Denkhaus, was also wounded, as were other unit personnel. The I. *Gruppe Stab* was forced to move to Hopsten, from where it subsequently rotated between Hörstel, Dreierwalde and Esch.

There was a change in leadership at the head of II./KG 51 on 9 November when the *Kommandeur*, Hauptmann Karl Egon *Freiherr* von Dalwigk zu Lichtenfels, was transferred to command I./JG 108 at Bad Vöslau. Hauptmann Hans-Joachim Grundmann took his place.

With improved weather on the 10th, by which time British, Canadian, Polish and US forces had cleared the area south of the Maas of all German resistance, Hauptmann Abrahamczik, Leutnant von Ritter-Rittershain, Oberfeldwebel Petersen and Leutnant Haeffner flew their first mission from Rheine against the bridges at Nijmegen. Their Me 262s were each loaded with two SD 250s. Haeffner experienced problems with his undercarriage soon after takeoff and fell behind, but the remaining three machines made it to the target. There, they encountered three patrolling Spitfires and were prevented from carrying out their mission. Haeffner, however, flew on alone through low-lying cloud and dropped both of his bombs on the bridge while coming under intense flak.

On this day, I./KG 51 (3. *Staffel*) reported ten Me 262s and ten pilots operationally ready, while Grundmann's II./KG 51 was 'equipping' at Schwäbisch Hall, having had a further 19 Me 262s assigned to it. The *Stab*/KG 51, under Major Unrau, was also 'equipping' at Landsberg, but so far it had just one Me 262 assigned!

Rudolf Abrahamczik flew an armed weather reconnaissance sortie during the morning of 11 November over the Helmond area, where he was fired on by strong flak. Despite this, he dropped his two SD 250s on positions held by the British Second Army. In the afternoon Batel, Haeffner and Oberfeldwebel Hans Kohler (the latter of 3./KG 51) flew via Venlo to attack Eindhoven airfield. Once again Haeffner was plagued by problems with his aircraft over Venlo and had to turn back. As he attempted to make for home, he observed a formation of Spitfires over Eindhoven

Major Heinz Unrau (kneeling at centre) listens to the injured Hauptmann Eberhard Winkel, *Kapitän* of 3./KG 51, over a cigarette at Rheine following his brush with Allied fighters on 2 November 1944. Standing with his left hand in his pocket at right is Oberleutnant Gustav Stephan, who would succeed Winkel as commander of 3. *Staffel* on 22 March 1945

Hauptmann Rudolf Abrahamczik, commander of 2./KG 51, warms his hands in the heat of a turbojet in the chill autumn air at Rheine in 1944. A holder of the Knight's Cross since February of that year, Abrahamczik would go on to see more operational flying in the Me 262 than most Luftwaffe jet pilots

and flew to the north, but became disorientated. Haeffner eventually dropped his two SD 250s on a troop column near Herzogenbosch.

An unnamed pilot of KG 51 captured by the Allies described what it was like to fly jet-bombing missions at this time;

'Briefing usually was very short, lasting from five to ten minutes. Information given was concerned only with the target, and its location. There was no orientation on flak or other factors affecting the mission. We were left to figure out our routes to and from the target, and the altitudes to be flown.

'The deepest penetration Me 262s made with bombs was 250 km flying at an altitude of 4000 m. The formation flown to the target was usually of four aircraft abreast, with 25-30 m between wingtips. Speed to the target was about 675 km/h. The usual altitude was 4000 m, and each aircraft carried two 250 kg bombs under the nose. Prior to January 1945, Hitler's personal order forbade any Me 262 flying below 4000 m. The serious effect of this flying altitude on bombing accuracy caused continuous complaints from the pilots, but it was not until the end of January that the order was changed to allow pilots to go down to an altitude they considered safe.

'When Allied fighters were encountered en route to the target, the Me 262s usually increased speed and easily climbed away. Flak was evaded rather easily by weaving from side-to-side. The maximum diving angle of the Me 262 with bombs was 35 degrees. We usually dived from 4000 m down to 1000 m, but never much lower. Care was taken to prevent the air speed exceeding 920 km/h, since the Me 262 was red-lined at 950 km/h. Care was also exercised to empty the rear 600-litre tank before the dive. This was necessary because the release of bombs with a full rear tank caused the nose of the aircraft to pitch up very suddenly, either knocking out the pilot or throwing the machine into an uncontrollable spin. Our pilots used the old *Revi* bombsight, which was supposedly accurate to within 35-40 m. Following release of our bombs, the Me 262s returned home at between 1000-1200 m, with a distance of 60-90 m between aircraft.'

On 19 November 1944, the bulk of personnel from 2./KG 51 finally arrived for operations at Hopsten from the unit's former base at Giebelstadt, while in the afternoon orders were issued to JG 27, whose Bf 109 fighters were assigned to conduct airfield defence for the Me 262s of KG 51. I./JG 27 was to cover Rheine, II./JG 27 Hopsten, III./JG 27 Hesepe and IV./JG 27 Achmer.

Between 1200-1300 hrs, Oberfeldwebel Otto Streit (a new arrival from 2. *Staffel*), Haeffner, Abrahamczik and Batel flew missions to Volkel, their aircraft carrying SD 250s. Six Spitfires were observed over the target area, but no contact ensued, and the Me 262s dropped their bombs and then returned to Hopsten individually.

19 November also saw II./KG 51 ordered to engage in operations in the Hürtgenwald. The unit prepared to transfer to Essen-Mühlheim, but because of the short runway there, operations were only possible with RATO units. However, it is doubtful

Fresh from visiting *Kommando Nowotny* at Achmer (which had just lost its illustrious commander, Major Walter Nowotny, to P-51 Mustangs), Generalleutnant Adolf Galland, the *General der Jagdflieger*, offers an encouraging pat on the shoulder to Major Heinz Unrau, commander of I./KG 51, at Hopsten in November 1944

that this transfer took place, for the next day II. *Gruppe* was still at Schwäbisch Hall, reporting that it had received 15 of its 40 allocated Ar 234 *Blitzbombers*. I./KG 51 reported 28 Me 262s on strength, while III./KG 51, in addition to its 14 Me 262s, had been assigned a single Ju 88, some Me 410s and a single Bf 109 and Fw 190 for training. Across the *Geschwader*, just 14 instructors had the task of training up to 116 pilots on the new type.

On 23 November KG 51, whose I. *Gruppe* had been removed from the control of *Luftwaffenkommando West*, was placed under the tactical control of *Generalmajor* Walter Grabmann's 3. *Jagddivision*. At some point during November, I./KG 51 was ordered to maintain at least one *Staffel* with jets armed with four 30 mm MK 108 cannon and II. *Gruppe* was ordered to endeavour to so equip all of its aircraft as well. This was probably in response to the increasing pressure to deploy even Me 262s of KG 51 against USAAF four-engined bombers attacking the Reich.

For the last ten days of the month KG 51 maintained a steady rate of operations, mostly it seems by 2. *Staffel*, against Allied ground forces from Roermond in the south to Nijmegen in the north. On the morning of the 21st Abrahamczik took off on the first of two missions to Nijmegen (accompanied by Hermann Wieczorek), where the pilots each dropped a pair of SD 250s. In the mid-afternoon, Abrahamczik led a *Kette* comprising Oberfeldwebel Wilhelm Kröfges and Feldwebel Karl-Albrecht Capitain (1. *Staffel*) against artillery positions around the town, again dropping SD 250s. The following day, Haeffner, Rösch and von Ritter-Rittershain bombed Nijmegen with good effect, despite poor visibility.

From 0936 hrs on the 26th, in what would be a busy day, KG 51 deployed five *Schwärme* of four Me 262s each from Hopsten in a wide-ranging operation, each carrying two SD 250s against enemy artillery positions at Roermond, Duerne, Nijmegen and Helmond. The first *Schwarm* was led by Abrahamczik, accompanied by Hauptmann Rudolf Rösch of 3. *Staffel*, together with 2./KG 51 pilots Capitain and Oberfeldwebel Erich Kaiser. The second *Schwarm* was led by von Ritter-Rittershain, accompanied by Petersen, Feldwebel Hans Meyer and Unteroffizier Heinz Werntgen, both of 2. *Staffel*, which was followed eight minutes after takeoff by the third *Schwarm*, led by Oberleutnant Heinz Lehmann (1. *Staffel*), along with Unteroffizere Horst Sanio, Joachim Kroll and Heinz Erben, all of 2. *Staffel*.

Next, at 1000 hrs, came the *Schwarm* led by Oberleutnant Heinz Strothmann, with Unteroffizier Eberhard Pöhling of 2./KG 51 and Leutnant Ernst Strate and Fahnenjunker-Feldwebel Hans-Robert Fröhlich, both from the *Erprobungsschwarm des Generals der Schlachtflieger* (Test Flight of the General of Ground-Attack Aviation). This small tactical development unit, consisting of just four pilots, was under the direct command of the *General der Schlachtflieger*, Oberst Hubertus Hitschhold, and was led by Major Heinrich Brücker

As dusk approaches, Me 262A-2a '9K+(red)BK' is towed by a *Kettenkrad* from its forest dispersal at Rheine in late 1944 in readiness for another mission over enemy lines. Camouflage and measures of concealment on German jet airfields were essential at this time as protection from marauding Allied fighters

CHAPTER THREE

who, until the summer of 1944, had been *Kommodore* of SG 4, before joining Hitschhold's staff. The unit's main task was to assess the Me 262 as a ground-attack aircraft, and to recommend the best methods for its tactical deployment.

Haeffner led the last *Schwarm*, consisting of 2./KG 51's Leutnant Hans Heid, Oberfeldwebel Otto Streit and Unteroffizier Ernst Altenheimer. Heid was forced to turn back because of undercarriage problems and Haeffner continued on to the target in bad weather accompanied only by Streit. By the time the jets reached the Maas, the pilots were flying blind. The weather prevented an attack on Venlo, so they tried to find Duerne, to the northwest, as an alternative target. Descending from 6000 m to 2000 m, both Me 262s dropped their bombs on artillery positions, but then encountered Spitfires and were forced to split up and return to Hopsten through thick cloud.

As he came into land just after 1100 hrs, Streit saw a burning Bf 109 on the runway. The alarm was sounded, and at that moment Tempests from No 3 Sqn attacked the airfield. Plt Off Bob Cole, who had shot down Edmund Delatowski on 13 October, was forced to take to his parachute after his fighter was hit by flak directly over the base.

Meanwhile, Leutnant von Ritter-Rittershain landed in Düsseldorf after running out of fuel, while Unteroffizier Kroll landed at Achmer. Unteroffizier Erben made an emergency landing near Plantlünne and Oberleutnant Lehmann crashed just south of Kirchwistedt, 20 km southeast of Bremerhaven. The final loss of the day was Unteroffizier Horst Sanio of 2./KG 51, who was shot down by British flak over Helmond. In four days 2./KG 51 had lost three pilots.

Also in action from Rheine on 26 November was Hauptmann Hans Gutzmer of the *Stab* KG 51, who was sent to attack enemy troop positions in Holland. That same day 6./KG 51 pilot Unteroffizier Martin Golde took off from Schwäbisch Hall to engage enemy fighters, but he returned after some 50 minutes without success.

On the 28th, I./KG 51 at Rheine and Hopsten reported a strength of 48 aircraft and 46 crews. However, during the course of the day Hauptmann Rösch of 3./KG 51 was reported missing during an armed meteorological reconnaissance flight west of Helmond, having been accompanied aloft by Hans Meyer. The two jets bombed Helmond, where they attracted anti-aircraft fire. At 1030 hrs Rösch's aircraft was hit, but he did not bail out and the jet crashed into the ground. Meyer returned home alone. Rudolf Rösch had been awarded the Knight's Cross in March 1944 after flying 100 missions in the Ju 88. One one occasion he had landed 80 km behind enemy lines in Russia to rescue the downed crew of his *Gruppenkommandeur*.

During the afternoon of 29 November, Hauptmann Gutzmer flew a lone attack over Holland

Pilots of I./KG 51 outside their battle HQ at Hopsten in late 1944. They are, from left to right, Leutnante Wilhelm Batel (Technical Officer), Heinrich Haeffner and von Ritter-Rittershain (latter two both from 2. *Staffel*), Hauptmann Rudolf Abrahamczik (*Kapitän* of 2. *Staffel*), Hauptmann Rudolf Rösch and Leutnant Albert Maser (both from 3. *Staffel*)

with two SD 250s, while Feldwebel Capitain took off from Hopsten to defend the airfield against enemy fighters operating in the immediate vicinity, but he was forced to return after ten minutes when his instruments failed. The next day Gutzmer flew another mission over Holland, again with two SD 250s.

Throughout November 1944 KG 51 had been assigned 33 jets, of which eight went to I. *Gruppe* and 23 to II./KG 51. By the end of the month bombing accuracy by the *Geschwader* was reported as being generally within 100 m of a target, but there were still familiarisation problems being experienced. These included the somewhat worrying and mysterious cases of poisoning and burns that were affecting a small number of pilots, including an Unteroffizier who died after developing only minor burns to his hands. J2 jet fuel was subsequently found to be the cause of these ailments.

Meanwhile, the beginning of December 1944 had seen the Luftwaffe's jet bomber force gradually expanding in size. The *Geschwader Stab* of KG 51, with six Me 262s, was operational at Rheine, as was most of the I. *Gruppe* (which also had aircraft at Hopsten). II./KG 51 was still undergoing training, reporting that it had reached its establishment of 36 aircraft – 22 at its base at Schwäbisch Hall and 14 in transit from Lechfeld. A total of 53 pilots was also reported available. The IV.(*Ergänzungs*) *Gruppe* – a training unit based at München-Riem under the command of Knight's Cross-holder Major Siegfried Barth (a veteran of the fighting over the Black Sea in 1942) – reported a strength of 109 pilots at this time.

On 2 December II./KG 51 reported 36 aircraft on strength, divided between Schwäbisch Hall and Lechfeld, together with 55 crews – all at Schwäbisch Hall. However, on that day Hauptmann Ernst Freistedt of 5./KG 51 was lost due to reasons unknown near Schwäbisch Hall when his Me 262A-2a was seen to dive suddenly into the ground. He was testing a new map-reading device at the time.

The morning of the 3rd was active operationally. Shortly before 0900 hrs, Rudolf Abrahamczik and Unteroffizier Walter Kolb of 2./KG 51 took off to bomb Nijmegen, but they were attacked by P-38s in the vicinity of the target and had to abandon the mission. Kolb made an emergency landing at Hilden, southeast of Dusseldorf, due to a shortage of fuel.

Altogether, I./KG 51 flew 30 sorties that day, including three operations when the *Gruppe's* Me 262s were used as fighters. Georg Csurusky, Karl-Albrecht Capitain, Leutnant Fritz Esche and Oberleutnant Hans-Joachim Valet (a Knight's Cross-holder and former transport pilot who had joined 1.*Staffel* from 3./TG 2) were scrambled from Rheine to intercept Allied fighters hawking over German airfields. Just after takeoff however, Capitain had to abandon his flight because of failure in the right turbine of his jet. As the remaining pilots manoeuvred to make

The wreckage of Unteroffizier Horst Sanio's Me 262A-2a Wk-Nr. 170229 '9K+JK' litters the countryside near Helmond and proves of interest to Allied military personnel. Sanio, of 2./KG 51, had been shot down by flak on 26 November 1944

CHAPTER THREE

Their faces showing the strain of air combat, three pilots of 1./KG 51 report to Major Heinz Unrau, *Gruppenkommandeur*, at Rheine on 3 December 1944. Feldwebel Werner Schmidt (centre of three pilots), who claimed the shooting down of a B-17 in the Rheine/Nordhorn area that day, is flanked to his right by Feldwebel Helmut Bruhn and, to his left, by Oberfeldwebel Erich Kaiser. Watching on is Oberfeldwebel Siegfried Prehl also of 1. *Staffel*

Knight's Cross-holder Oberleutnant Hans-Joachim Valet of 1./KG 51 (centre with back to camera) joins Oberleutnant Ludwig Albersmeyer (left – Operations Officer of I. *Gruppe*) and Oberleutnant Georg Csurusky (*Kapitän* of 1./KG 51) for breakfast in their quarters. Valet was killed on 3 December 1944 when his Me 262 was attacked by a Tempest over Rheine as he made a landing approach

an attack on an enemy formation, Csurusky lost sight of Valet, his *Rottenflieger*. This was because he too had suffered engine failure and been forced to return to base.

As Valet made his approach to Rheine, a Tempest came in behind him piloted by Flt Lt J W Garland of No 80 Sqn, who was flying an armed reconnaissance. The RAF pilot had spotted the Me 262 southeast of Rheine and immediately applied full throttle, closing quickly. As he approached to within firing range, the jet suddenly turned to port and shed its canopy. Tightening its turn, the Me 262 flick-rolled into the ground from about 30 m and crashed. Although Garland could not remember whether he had actually opened fire, he was credited with the victory nevertheless.

Esche also experienced high drama during the mission, being forced to land at Hopsten with a burning engine unit following an attack on a pair of P-47s.

That day, I./KG 51 pilots accounted for what was thought to have been either a B-24 Liberator or a Lancaster shot down (although RAF Bomber Command recorded no losses on 3 December).

An Me 262A-1a fighter was damaged at a 'training airfield' on the 3rd while undertaking a bomb-carrying trial piloted by the *Kommandeur* of II. *Gruppe*, Hauptmann Grundmann.

That same day a KG 51 advanced detachment at Hesepe expressed its concern to a higher command about the paucity of supplies at the airfield, as well as the basic servicing facilities. The detachment felt that this situation was only going to get worse in view of the fact that 6. *Staffel* – at least – was apparently on the verge of moving north to Hesepe. The next day this *Staffel* was told to get its supplies from *Luftgau* XI, which controlled Hesepe, suggesting that at least its ground elements had arrived there.

At midday on 5 December, Feldwebel Capitain was again scrambled to engage Allied fighters but his undercarriage failed to function as he took off and he was forced to land just seven minutes later, suffering 20 per cent damage to his aircraft. At 1233 hrs, Leutnant Esche and Feldwebel Werner Schmidt, both of 1./KG 51 and flying Me 262A-1as, were ordered into the air on a fighter operation in the Rheine-Münster-Osnabrück area. Thirty minutes later, despite experiencing engine problems, Schmidt attacked a lone B-17 of the 91st BG between Rheine and Nordhorn. The bomber began to burn and Schmidt counted six crewmen bail out. The B-17 struck the ground near Lingen.

Generalmajor Dietrich Peltz, commander of II. *Jagdkorps*, held a special course at Rheine in early December at which new tactics were worked out with a view to I./KG 51 taking over all of of II.*Gruppe's* four-cannon Me 262s so as to be completely equipped with the 'bomber-fighter' type. For the first time orders were issued for the jets to attempt to engage and break up Allied fighter and bomber formations while avoiding direct combat.

On 7 December Hauptmann Csurusky and Oberfeldwebel Erich Kaiser of 1./KG 51 took off on a mid-morning patrol. In the vicinity of Stuttgart, Csurusky spotted a formation of Spitfires and manoeuvred to launch an attack, but whilst doing so, at a range of 200 metres, he discovered to his horror that his guns had jammed and he was forced to dive under the enemy fighters and then climb away. This manoeuvre served to alarm the Spitfire pilots sufficiently, and Csurusky observed with relief that the Allied fighters had broken formation and scattered.

Just after 0800 hrs the next morning, Hauptmann Gutzmer flew a lone sortie from Hopsten over Holland in a jet armed with two SD 250s and returned safely – a mission he repeated the next day. Oberfeldwebel Ernst Peters of 2. *Staffel* was not so fortunate, however. As he returned from a mission on the 8th, his aircraft crash-landed and burst into flames. Peters suffered third-degree burns and was hospitalised.

The following day P-51 pilot Lt Harry L Edwards of the 352nd FG intercepted an Me 262 at about 29,000 ft in the Kirchheim-am-Ries area. He fired a long burst, knocking out one of the jet's engines. The German pilot, Stabsfeldwebel Hans Zander of 4./KG 51, then dived towards the ground, but after levelling off at 500 ft, Edwards was able to fire another burst, shooting large pieces off the jet. As he pulled up, the Me 262A-2a crashed into the ground and exploded in two sheets of flame at Zimmerbach, north of Schwäbish-Gmund. Zander perished.

During the mid-afternoon of 10 December, Gutzmer, Abrahamczik and Oberfeldwebel Wieczorek all mounted attacks on Nijmegen with SD 250s, although Abrahamczik had to abort due to R/T failure and Wieczorek completed the mission alone.

Two aircraft from 3./KG 51 were lost that afternoon, Feldwebel Herbert Lenk being shot down south of Wierden by flak and Leutnant Walter Roth falling victim to RAF fighters. The latter had attempted to bounce a Tempest from No 56 Sqn over Bevergern, east of Rheine. A second Tempest, flown by Flt Sgt L Jackson, then turned into the jet and pursued it in a 420-mph dive. Roth levelled out at 14,000 ft and Jackson opened fire, scoring hits on the starboard side of the fuselage. Roth escaped into cloud and made an emergency landing, although he was injured in the process.

That evening II./KG 51 reported a reduced strength of 34 aircraft and 52 crews.

While flying an operation in the Aachen area on 12 December, Oberfeldwebel Hans Kohler of 3./KG 51 was posted missing. He may have been the victim of Allied fighters. Three days later orders were issued to 4. and 5./KG 51 to move by road to Achmer, with the *Gruppenstab* moving to Hesepe. The flying elements were to transfer as weather allowed.

Oberfeldwebel Erich Kaiser of 1./KG 51 checks the nose of his Me 262 prior to an operation. On 3 January 1945 Kaiser succumbed to spinal injuries (in hospital at Lingen) that he had suffered following an emergency landing after the mission to attack Eindhoven airfield as part of Operation *Bodenplatte* on New Year's Day. A veteran airman, the 30-year-old Kaiser had flown 300 missions and was a recipient of the German Cross in Gold

The last great German offensive in the West began at 0530 hrs on 16 December 1944. It was a plan so audacious that no senior Allied commander expected it. Codenamed *Wacht-am-Rhein*, the offensive was devised by Hitler, who wanted to drive an armoured wedge between the Allies by thrusting through the forests and hill country of the Ardennes to retake Antwerp. He also hoped that he could trap the US First and Ninth Armies around Aachen, thus eliminating the threat posed to the Ruhr.

As SS-*Oberstgruppenführer* Josef 'Sepp' Dietrich's 6. *Panzer Armee* drove west, encircling Bastogne and trapping several thousand American troops, initially the Allied air forces remained largely grounded by bad weather. To succeed, however, it was vital for the Germans to have as much air support as possible. As part of this support, a small component of six Me 262s from II./KG 51 was ordered to transfer by road to Hesepe and Achmer under the command of Hauptmann Grundmann.

At the beginning of the Ardennes offensive, *Luftwaffenkommando West* reported that the *Stab*, I. *Gruppe* and 6. *Staffel* had 42 Me 262s on strength.

On 17 December, I./KG 51 went into action when six Me 262s strafed US troops in the St Vith area. Away from the Ardennes, at 0749 hrs Gutzmer took off from Rheine and attacked targets in Holland with a pair of SD 250s. He landed at Achmer, where some ground elements of II. *Gruppe* were now based. He was followed by Abrahamczik and Wieczorek, who left Hopsten at 1000 hrs to attack enemy columns near Bree. Three minutes later, Esche and Capitain of 1. *Staffel* took off to bomb the railway station at Moll, 50 km east of Antwerp. Heid took off at 1037 hrs to strike at enemy columns on a stretch of road between Peer, northeast of Beringen, and Bree. His SD 250 *Splitterbomben* hit the target, despite Heid's Me 262 having attracted attention from both enemy fighters and flak batteries.

In the afternoon, the duo of Abrahamczik and Wieczorek, accompanied by Haeffner, were airborne again from Hopsten to attack enemy forces on the road between Eindhoven and Hasselt. The jet pilots had to use their blind-flying skills en route to the target, and when they arrived over the target area, they were met by very heavy flak. All three Me 262s returned safely, however.

As indicated, the move ordered on 15 December had by now begun. The strength of II. *Gruppe* was 28 jets – 18 divided between Schwäbisch Hall and Lechfeld, with six at either Hopsten or Hesepe and one believed to be at Kassel-Rothwesten. There were 51 crews. The *Gruppe* lost its first Me 262A-2a to enemy action on 17 December when Leutnant Wolfgang Lübcke of 6. *Staffel* was shot down over Hesepe airfield.

The weather the following day was bad. Despite this, Hauptmann Gutzmer managed to make a reconnaissance flight from Achmer. He would be in the air again that afternoon when he attacked enemy positions in the Ardennes around Bastogne. Shortly after 1000 hrs, Feldwebel Capitain took off to bomb a factory at Lammersdorf, southeast of Aachen, with two SC 250s. Capitain observed his bombs hit to good effect. And despite the adverse conditions, the intrepid Abrahamczik also took off to attack enemy columns near Weert.

I./KG 51 reported that 20 Me 262 sorties had been flown on 18 December, 18 jets taking off between 0744 hrs and 0818 hrs. A further two aircraft sortied at 1110 hrs, their task being to tie down Allied fighters in the battle area and to harass troop movements. No Allied aircraft were encountered and no losses suffered. Targets included vehicles north of Hasselt and Neerpelt railway station. Two aircraft broke off owing to technical failures and another one force-landed. Two jets on a meteorological reconnaissance mission also had to abort owing to bad weather, but they did at least report a strengthening of light flak. Generally, it was considered that there were very few worthwhile targets.

On the 19th Gutzmer led a formation of Me 262s flown by pilots on their first mission. The aircraft were sent to strafe targets in the Liège area, and no other details are known about this operation. Gutzmer attacked the same targets on the 20th. The following day Schenck asked Hans-Joachim Grundmann, *Kommandeur* of II./KG 51, why the transfer of the remaining elements of his *Gruppe* had not been executed, and why the *Stab* was being held back at Schwäbisch Hall?

5./KG 51 reported serious damage to one of its jets on 22 December following a formation flight near Schwäbisch Hall. That evening, a message was flashed stating that 4. and 5. *Staffeln* would land at Achmer, but this appears to have been advance notice for the next day. It seems that most of the groundcrew had already departed Schwäbisch Hall by this point and were in place at Achmer and Hesepe. However, Grundmann signalled Schenck from Schwäbisch Hall stating that he needed another 200 men to help service the aircraft there, as well as to guard them since 'cases of sabotage have occurred here'. Furthermore, the factories could not assist in making the *Gruppe's* aircraft serviceable as they had too many of their own to attend to. The *Gruppe Stab* would move when a supply of aircraft had been arranged and Grundmann had been transferred by air.

Finally, on 23 December, the fog lifted and Allied air superiority was quickly re-established. The rail system upon which the German commanders in the Ardennes were so dependent for their supplies was subjected to attack by Allied bombers. Hardly a train got through from the railway yards in Germany without being attacked, and 'Sepp' Dietrich's tanks were slowly starved of fuel. Simultaneously, P-38 and P-47 fighter-bombers of the US Ninth Air Force began a systematic ground-attack campaign in support of recovering Allied ground forces.

Its canopy open, an Me 262 of 1./KG 51 taxies in at a damp Hopsten following the completion of a mission at dusk in late 1944

However, KG 51 – either I. or II. *Gruppe* – reported it impossible 'to take off because of bad visibility' on 23 December, but that 'readiness was assured'. The same day, the *Stab* informed II. *Gruppe* that 12 Me 262s had been allocated – eight for II. *Gruppe* and four for I. *Gruppe*. The latter were to be assembled at Lechfeld and II. *Gruppe* aircraft at Schwäbisch Hall.

Unteroffizier Axel von Zimmermann of 6./KG 51 was killed at Hessental, near Schwäbisch Hall, on Christmas Eve when his jet crashed during a ferry flight.

At this time many radio signals were being exchanged between Schenck and Grundmann of II./KG 51. Schenck was asking the *Gruppenkommandeur* once again why the remainder of II. *Gruppe* had not yet transferred to its operational bases. On this day, Schenck ordered that 6. *Staffel* was to move its ground elements and signals platoon to Bonn-Hangelar, the latter to be in place by Christmas Day. Also at this time, nine Me 262s of KG 51 were transferred to III./JG 7 at Parchim and 16 aircraft to I./KG 54 at Giebelstadt.

On Christmas morning II./KG 51 was told peremptorily that weather conditions for transfer were unusually favourable in spite of the ground mist, and that turning back on account of bands of fog was unjustified. The *Gruppe* personnel showed great reluctance to move, however. At the same time, Batel, the Technical Officer of I./KG 51, informed the *General der Kampfflieger* that I. *Gruppe* and elements of II./KG 51, which had arrived in the operations area, would report strengths daily to II. *Jagdkorps*.

On Christmas Day the main target for KG 51 was Liège. The jet of Oberleutnant Hans-Georg Lamle, *Staffelführer* of 4./KG 51, was initially hit by British flak while in the target area near Liège, and then on his return to base he was intercepted by a Spitfire from No 411 Sqn RCAF near Heesch. The pilot, future ace Flt Lt Jack Boyle, later reported;

'As we neared our home base at Heesch, we were far too high and in an irritable mood. To get rid of excess height, I stuck the nose almost straight down in a screaming spiral dive. As my speed shot past 500 mph, a German Me 262 appeared out of nowhere. It only took a second to see to my gunsight and safety catch and I was right behind him. My first burst of cannon fire hit his port engine pod and it began streaming dense smoke. He immediately dove for the deck as an evasive tactic, but with only one engine, he couldn't outrun me. I scored several more hits before he clipped some tall treetops and then hit the ground at an almost flat angle. His aircraft disintegrated in stages from nose to tail as it ripped up the turf for several hundred yards until only the tail assembly was left, and it went cartwheeling along just below me at about my speed.'

Lamle's jet had hit the ground near Erp, 107 km north of Liège.

About three hours later, four Spitfires from No 403 Sqn RCAF, flying a patrol along the Rhine, spotted three enemy aircraft 2000 ft above them. As they climbed to intercept, it became obvious to the Canadians that they were Me 262s. Catching all three jets completely by surprise, Sqn Ldr James Collier, leading the Spitfires, was able to open fire on the lead jet, flown by Feldwebel Hans Meyer of 2./KG 51, from about 70 yards. The starboard engine of the Me 262A-1a burst into flames and it went into a steep dive. Meyer, who was flying with

Oberfeldwebel Wieczorek on a mission to Liège, bailed out near Eupin but was killed.

Liège was targeted by KG 51 again on the 27th, but there were also further missions to Nijmegen, where Feldwebel Johann 'Hans' Trenke of 6./KG 51, despite heavy flak, made a gliding attack and dropped two bombs into the town. His *Staffel* comrade, Fahnenjunker-Oberfeldwebel Wilhelm Haase, also attempted to reach Nijmegen but ran into enemy fighters. Haase managed to evade them, however, and instead attacked Allied troop targets on the Hasselt-Zonhoven road.

Both Trenke and Heinrich Haeffner flew multiple sorties that day, Trenke to Hasselt and Haeffner twice to Liège. During a fighter sweep in the Rheine area, a Spitfire piloted by Flg Off M A Perkins of No 442 Sqn RCAF claimed an Me 262 damaged. This may have been the aircraft flown by Feldwebel Walter Wehking of 4./KG 51, which crashed near Bünde/Westfalen. Wehking bailed out. An Allied radio decrypt reported that part of II./KG 51 had arrived at Hesepe and that a jet had crashed, its pilot being taken to hospital at Bielefeld. This was probably Wehking.

It was proposed that II./KG 51 should eventually become fully operational at Essen-Mühlheim. Ground elements of the *Gruppe* had by then started to receive training in 'close combat anti-tank fighting', the *Stab* company's training being complete, with 4., 5. and 6. *Staffel* due to start. Some aircraft still remained at Schwäbisch Hall and Lechfeld, but these probably formed a reserve pool for the whole of KG 51, consisting of six jets – including two at Schwäbisch Hall (where there were 29 crews) and one at Lechfeld.

Hampered by Allied air power, weather and terrain, starved of fuel and meeting firm opposition, the German assault in the Ardennes, having penetrated 112 kilometres at its deepest point, was still far short of Antwerp when it faltered and stopped on 30 December 1944. That day the last attempt to close the Bastogne corridor failed, and with the initiative now lost, *General der Panzertruppe* Hasso Eccard von Manteuffel's 5. *Panzer Armee* abandoned any hope of further offensive action.

The Luftwaffe Quartermaster at Gütersloh was placed on readiness to make sure that 'pretty large quantities of J2 [fuel]' would be available by 10 January 1945 for the arrival of Grundmann and II./KG 51. On 31 December the Quartermaster was informed that the 1600-metre runway at Essen-Mühlheim would not be ready before 6 January, and it was agreed that the unit would not arrive before the 10th. But as the new year of 1945 dawned, all these plans would be placed in abeyance by an audacious and unexpected operation in which the Luftwaffe would gamble its precious stocks of strike aircraft and cadres of pilots in a determined attempt to cripple Allied tactical air power on the ground – and KG 51 would be required to play its part.

Personnel of I./KG 51 do their best to enjoy what would be the unit's last wartime Christmas dinner. From left to right are Oberleutnant Harald Hovestadt (*Gruppe Adjutant*), Major Heinz Unrau (*Gruppenkommandeur*) and Inspektor Hans Hoiß (*Stab* administration). Hovestadt would be badly injured on 13 March 1945 when shot down by enemy fighters during a mission to attack Allied vehicles near Kalkar

HIGH-SPEED INTELLIGENCE

Aside from the bomber variant of the Me 262, as early as September 1941 the RLM had been attracted by the notion of a jet-powered reconnaissance aircraft, or *Aufklärer*. The following month Messerschmitt duly supplied a preliminary proposal for an unarmed version of the Me 262 that would carry two Rb (*Reihenbilder*) 50/30 (50 cm lens) cameras – models which had been designed as commercial mapping cameras intended for peacetime use in straight-and-level flight. This outline was reviewed in February 1942 when the RLM, having examined a wooden mock-up, suggested the installation of Rb 75/30 (75 cm lens) cameras and FuG 16Z or EZ6 radio equipment.

Later, as part of the August 1943 design proposals described in Chapter 1, Messerschmitt proposed further Me 262 variants known as the *Aufklärer* I, Ia and II. In the unarmed *Aufklärer* I, a 500-litre fuel tank was to be installed in the jet's nose, with either one Rb 75/30 and one Rb 20/30, dating from 1938, or a pair of angled Rb 75/30 cameras fitted behind this tank. The camera lenses would be covered by glazed panels. The 250-litre tank below the pilot's seat was removed, but a new 750-litre tank was to be built into the central fuselage section.

Like the *Schnellbomber* Ia, the armed *Aufklärer* Ia saw cockpit and radio equipment moved forward to the nose, and the aircraft had a fuel capacity of 3000 litres. Camera provision was to have come in the form of two Rb 75/30s in the rear fuselage and armament from two 30 mm MK 108 cannon in the nose. Finally, the *Aufklärer* II bore a strong resemblance to the *Schnellbomber* II, with a bulbous fuselage carrying 5200 litres of fuel. Because of fuel load, its nose-mounted Rb 20/30 and two Rb 75/30s, this variant carried no weapons. There was a plan to accommodate a second crew member, but this idea was later withdrawn.

Eventually, it was decided to return to Messerschmitt's original proposal, as per a 1942 wooden mock-up, and develop the Me 262A-5a reconnaissance jet. Until such time as the aircraft had been tested and proven in combat, however, the reconnaissance role would be performed by an interim variant – the Me 262A-1a/U3 *Behelfsaufklärer* – which was a modification of a standard fighter.

This design would feature two Rb 50/30 cameras in the nose, angled outwards at 11 degrees, controlled by an intervalometer with an attached drive motor. The cameras were too large to install cleanly within the nose compartment, so small horizontal teardrop fairings were fitted to both left and right gun access panels to cover the protruding areas and the usual gun ports found on the A-1a were faired over. Two small square glazed panels were provided for the camera lenses beneath the fuselage on either side of the nosewheel well. The variant also incorporated a

FuG 16 ZS radio transceiver that operated on German army frequencies, and the aircraft had a single MK 108 cannon mounted in the extreme nose, with its muzzle protruding level with the tip.

Thanks to its superior speed in comparison to Allied fighters, the Me 262 was an ideal aircraft to provide short-range reconnaissance.

In June 1944 Oberleutnant Herward Braunegg was ordered to set up an experimental jet reconnaissance unit. Establishment of *Kommando Braunegg* began quickly at Lechfeld that summer.

Braunegg was a native of Graz who had joined the Austrian air force in September 1937. When this was incorporated into the German Luftwaffe following the *Anschluss* of March 1938, Braunegg attended the *Luftkriegschule* at Berlin-Gatow, before training with various *Aufklärungsfliegersschulen*.

In December 1939 he joined 1.(H)/41 and then 4.(H)/41. Serving in Russia, Braunegg was a unit HQ officer with the *Stab Nahaufklarungsgruppe* (NAG – Short-Range Reconnaissance Group) 9 from 15 June 1942 until the end of September of that year, when he was attached to the *Stab* IV. *Fliegerkorps* as an operations staff officer during the fighting in Stalingrad and in the Donets basin. Braunegg then returned to NAG 9 as Technical Officer and then as a *Staffelkapitän*, and he was awarded the Knight's Cross on 26 March 1944.

Two months later, on 29 May, Braunegg was placed in command of a *Sonderkommando* charged with assessing new aircraft, which brought him into contact with the Bf 109 and Me 262 at Lechfeld in June 1944. In total, Braunegg would fly 353 operational missions during the war.

Kommando Braunegg was formed with a cadre of four pilots – Oberleutnant Schlüter, the former Technical Officer of NAG 13, Oberleutnant Engelhart from NAG 9 and Oberleutnant Kopf and

An RAF leading aircraftsman examines a German Zeiss Rb 50/30 camera and film magazine fitted into its mounting frame. The camera featured a 50 cm lens with an iris inter-lens shutter. The magazine contained 64 m of film, and when loaded the whole camera and frame weighed a hefty 72 kg

With considerable experience from the Eastern Front, the Austrian Knight's Cross-holder Oberleutnant Herward Braunegg was appointed to lead the first *Sonderkommando* tasked with flying and evaluating the Me 262 as a reconnaissance and photo-reconnaissance aircraft under operational conditions. The small unit would carry his name as *Kommando Braunegg,* later known as *Kommando Panther*

Fahnenjunker-Oberfeldwebel Friedrich Stannek from 4.(H)/12, the latter a Knight's Cross-holder.

On 9 July Braunegg took delivery of Me 262A-1a/U3 Wk-Nr. 170006 'White 1' at Leipheim, into which two Rb 50/30s had been installed. This was the first Me 262 believed to have been converted to this variant, and Braunegg flew it to Lechfeld. On the 26th he flew 'White 1' from here on the first dedicated trial photo mission, and continued with similar assessment sorties over the coming weeks through to mid-September.

The plan was for *Kommando Braunegg* to trial the limited numbers of reconnaissance jets being produced, before confirming them as operationally ready to the *Versuchsverband* OKL (the Luftwaffe High Command's trials and research unit), which was to assume administrative control of the jets. From a day-to-day operational perspective, however, the *Kommando* remained independent. It would not be until 26 August that the first Me 262 reconnaissance machine was reported fully ready, and indeed, for the rest of its brief existence, the *Kommando* would operate a mixture of standard Me 262A-1as and a small number of modified A-1a/U3s.

On 25 October the *Kommando* suffered a major loss when 'White 1', piloted by Fahnenjunker-Oberfeldwebel Friedrich Stannek, crashed southeast of Lissa, in the province of Posen, while on a ferry flight from Schneidemühl to Lechfeld. Stannek was killed.

By 6 November *Kommando Braunegg* had three Me 262s on strength. That day Braunegg, Engelhart and Schlüter, together with a mobile photographic development facility and some groundcrew taken over from NAG 9, transferred from Lechfeld to Rheine. Oberleutnant Kopf remained as a 'rearguard' at Lechfeld. Simultaneously, Major Friedrich Heinz Schultze, on the staff of Generalmajor Karl-Henning von Barsewisch (the *General der Aufklärer*), issued orders for NAG 6 to reform as a short-range jet reconnaissance *Gruppe*. On 5 August the 'new' NAG 6 was created from elements of reconnaissance units that had previously seen operations on the southern sector of the Eastern Front and around Stalingrad. 1./NAGr 6 was formed at Bayreuth-Bindlach from 3.(H)/Aufkl.Gr.21 and 2./NAGr 6 at the same location from 12./Aufkl.Gr.12.

Following the death of the famous fighter ace Walter Nowotny while flying an Me 262 jet fighter of *Kommando Nowotny* on 8 November and injuries suffered by Oberleutnant Horst Götz of the Ar 234 jet reconnaissance unit *Kommando Götz*, it was decided to give the new jet trials units alternative names. Therefore, at the end of November 1944, *Kommando Braunegg* received the new designation *Kommando Panther*. By 28 November *Kommando Braunegg/Panther* had six Me 262s, with three serviceable, and four pilots. Two days later it transferred from Lechfeld to Schwäbisch Hall to operate under 5. *Jagddivision*.

In mid-December 1944 Oberleutnant Braunegg set up a battle HQ for his *Kommando* at the *Schloss* in the Hohenloher forest at Langenburg, northeast of Schwäbisch Hall. The HQ was placed under the command of Oberleutnant Erich Weiss, a former comrade from NAG 9. Oberleutnant Schlüter oversaw photographic development and motor transport, and the technicians who performed these tasks, while a

Me 262A-1a/U3 'White 3', attached to III./EJG 2 at Lechfeld in the spring of 1945, was used to conduct photo-reconnaissance trials before being handed over to NAG 6. The aircraft's usual gun access panels are open to reveal the replacement installation of twin Rb 50/30 cameras. Note also the single Mk 108 cannon barrel protruding from the tip of the nose – the area to which the weapon had been moved

signals detachment was established under Leutnant Mattick. The unit also had medical and meteorological officers.

For tactical purposes, the *Kommando* would operate under the command of 15. *Fliegerdivision*, and it was to fly photo and visual reconnaissance missions in cooperation with *Heeresgruppe Oberrhein* (Army Group Upper Rhine) over the Western Front.

By this time the unit had seven Me 262s on strength, which had been fitted with cameras at Schwäbisch Hall, while a further ten aircraft were being so equipped at Lechfeld.

Kommando Panther would play an important part in the preparations for the *Wacht-am-Rhein* counter-offensive in the Ardennes. The unit's aircraft were able to roam virtually at will over Allied lines, gathering vital photographic coverage of enemy troop dispositions and the crossings over the Meuse. On 15 December, the *Kommando* reported a strength of eleven pilots and six Me 262A-1a/U3s. Despite this, it was rare for more than four aircraft to be operational at any one time.

Missions seem to have started in earnest on the 17th when two *Rotten* of Me 262s flew a reconnaissance sortie over Allied lines. Next day, the *Kommando* was ordered to fly reconnaissance missions over the Trier-Saarbrücken-Lauterbourg area, and on the 22nd it mounted four sorties in the Mühlhausen-Basel-Delle-Weissenburg-Lautenburg-Bitsch areas. Three more sorties were flown on the 24th in the Saarlautern area.

By the end of the year the *General der Aufklärer* had proposed to equip NAG 1 with the Me 262, and the RLM had cancelled the proposed high-performance/high-altitude Bf 109H-2/R2 reconnaissance-fighter in favour of the Me 262A-1a/U3.

In late December Generalmajor von Barsewisch reported the following status – *Kommando Braunegg* operational under *Luftflotte West*, *Stab*/NAG 6 with Me 262s and Bf 110s non-operational under *Luftflotte Reich* and 1. and 2./NAG 6 non-operational under *Luftflotte 10*.

It had been, admittedly, a low-key start to Luftwaffe reconnaissance operations with the Me 262, but the value of these small units would be very much realised in the coming months when the intelligence that they provided to the German military high command, and its commanders in the field, would be rated extremely highly.

BODENPLATTE TO THE BANKS OF THE RHINE

On 5 December 1944, in the quiet village of Flammersfeld on the fringes of the Rhein-Westerwald, the CO of II. *Jagdkorps*, Generalmajor Dietrich Peltz, presided over a highly secret meeting of nearly all regional *Jagdführer* and fighter *Kommodore* on the Western Front. Supported by an increasingly despondent Göring, Peltz had decided that the best way to support operations in the Ardennes was to neutralise Allied tactical air power where it was at its most vulnerable – on the ground. By using the element of surprise, Peltz concluded that as an alternative to costly dogfights against numerically superior enemy fighter formations, such an attack would incur minimum casualties and consume less fuel. Originally intended to coincide with the launch of the ground offensive in the Ardennes, the weather had frustrated the plan, and the operation – known as *Bodenplatte* – was deferred, despite the commencement of *Wacht-am-Rhein*.

Peltz told his audience that at first light, under complete radio silence on a day when meteorological conditions were favourable, and guided by Ju 88 nightfighters acting as pathfinders, virtually the entire strength of the Luftwaffe's single-engined daylight fighter force on the Western Front would be deployed in a low-level attack against 11 key Allied fighter airfields across Belgium, Holland and northeastern France.

To conduct reconnaissance of the enemy airfields after the attack, Peltz turned to I./KG 51. Within four days of the Flammersfeld conference Oberstleutnant Schenck had been briefed, and he subsequently prepared instructions for his unit's involvement in the operation. In addition to 'confronting the enemy fighter response, and in that way covering the return of our own forces', the *Gruppe* was to obtain 'pictures of the parked aircraft', with the 'main goal' of the mission being coverage of the 'results of the fighter units'.

In accordance with instructions issued to other units, signalling of the codeword *'Varus'* would indicate that the operation was to take place within 24 hours, and that the maximum number of jets were to be made ready. *'Teutonicus'* indicated that aircraft were to be pulled to the edge of the field the evening before the attack, followed by *'Hermann'*, which would give the exact date and time of the attack. Pilots were to be notified of the unit's receipt of the codewords by Schenck himself. He also instructed that;

In the freezing air of a winter's morning, mechanics service the turbo units of Me 262s from I./KG 51, probably at Hopsten in late December 1944 or early 1945. This would have been the scene on the morning of 1 January 1945 when the Luftwaffe launched Operation *Bodenplatte*

Pilots and groundcrew of I./KG 51 struggle to keep warm in the cold air and mist of an early winter's morning at Hopsten in late December 1944 or early 1945. Behind them are Me 262s of 1. *Staffel* with their white-tipped noses, but they do not appear to be 'bombed up'

'Altitudes will be determined by weather conditions. However, in the interest of range, maximum altitude will be permitted during the approach. For the same reason, aircraft will be flown throttled back until contact with the enemy is made. It is possible that weather conditions will require an approach at low level. With a low-level approach, flights should avoid main roads over friendly territory and villages in the front areas. Times and course headings are to be memorised and compasses and watches are to be continually observed. Additionally, natural markers along the route are to be observed and followed to aid orientation.

'In order to obtain complete photographic coverage (overlapping), every pilot will be tasked with the reconnaissance of two airfields, with one being the main point of concentration. If contact is made with the enemy, reconnaissance photos are still to be taken. It is part of the mission to attack and shoot down enemy aircraft in order to prevent the pursuit of friendly forces. Due to the massing of friendly forces it will be easy to mistake friendly for enemy aircraft. Particular care must be taken to avoid such mistakes.

'Bombs [two 250 kg weapons per aircraft], carried for reasons of weight distribution, are to be dropped on enemy flak positions.

'Landings, beside at home airfields, can be made at Bonn-Hangelar. Landing at Odendorf is to be avoided since the camouflage and maintenance facilities are minimal. Lost aircraft are to locate the River Rhine and fly up- and downstream until the correct location is determined and the closest airfield is located, especially if fuel is low.'

The four commanders of I./KG 51. They are, from left to right, Hauptmann Eberhard Winkel (*Kapitän* of 3. *Staffel*), Oberleutnant Georg Csurusky (commanding 1. *Staffel*), Hauptmann Rudolf Abrahamczik (leading 2. *Staffel*) and, clutching several flight route maps, Major Heinz Unrau (*Gruppenkommandeur*)

Veteran pilot Oberfeldwebel Erich Kaiser of 1./KG 51 checks his course on a map. Following the execution of Operation *Bodenplatte* on 1 January 1945, he was forced to make an emergency landing that ultimately resulted in his death

Pilots were further instructed to evade capture at all costs if forced to bail out.

The first suitable break in the weather was forecast for dawn on 1 January 1945. KG 51's groundcrews worked throughout New Year's Eve to bring all their aircraft to readiness, while the pilots were ordered to their beds by 0030 hrs at the very latest. Shortly after 0600 hrs on New Year's morning, Major Unrau briefed his men and issued maps with details of their targets, enemy flak battery positions and navigational plans, while the *Staffelkapitäne* handled the reconnaissance requirements.

Following receipt of the *'Teutonicus'* and *'Hermann'* signals, German fighters from 33 *Gruppen* left their forward bases and headed in tight formation across the snow-covered landscape towards the Allied lines during the early morning. Although complete surprise was achieved and moderate success gained at Eindhoven (where two Canadian Typhoon squadrons were virtually destroyed), Brussels and St Denis-Westrem, the attacks on Antwerp, Le Culot and Volkel were nothing short of catastrophic.

Twenty-one Me 262s from I./KG 51 struck at Eindhoven and Gilze-Rijen – by far the largest effort so far mounted by the unit (the *Gruppe* had reported 21 aircraft out of 30 as serviceable on 31 December, with 33 pilots). Oberleutnant Haeffner of 2./KG 51 recalled;

'Reveille was at 0600 hrs, and just afterwards we assembled at headquarters. Our target was Gilze-Rijen. We were given reconnaissance photos to study while we waited for our "X-time". Takeoff was at 0855 hrs. The engines of the aircraft of both our *Gruppenkommandeur*, Major Unrau, and *Staffelkapitän*, Oberleutnant Abrahamczik, failed to start. Therefore, I had to lead the *Staffel* to the target. Near Arnhem, 15 enemy fighters [probably Spitfires from No 442 Sqn RCAF] attacked us, but we managed to evade them.

'After approaching the target, we quickly dived from 9000 m down to 1000 m and dropped our bombs. We then strafed the parked aircraft at low level. I flew once more over the field, taking photographs of the burning aeroplanes and wrecked hangars with my Robot camera. During the flight back to base I overflew Volkel airfield, where I saw at least 16 destroyed aircraft, taking more photographs. I landed safely at Hopsten at 0951 hrs.'

Recent research indicates that, altogether, nearly 300 Allied aircraft were destroyed as a result of *Bodenplatte*, of which some 145 were single-engined fighters. Another 180 aircraft were damaged and 185 personnel killed or wounded. *Bodenplatte* was, without doubt, an unexpected and painful blow for the 2nd TAF, but the effect on Allied tactical operations would be negligible.

In total, 143 German pilots were killed or reported missing, including three *Geschwaderkommodore*, five *Gruppenkommandeure* and 14 *Staffelkapitäne*, with a further 21 pilots wounded and 70 captured. Despite these losses, all of I./KG 51's aircraft returned unscathed. However, 1. *Staffel* pilot Oberfeldwebel Erich Kaiser had to make an emergency landing in his Me 262A-1a on the Wietmarscher Moor due to a lack of fuel. The aircraft was badly damaged and Kaiser suffered severe spinal injuries, which he succumbed to two days later.

I./KG 51's attack on Gilze-Rijen had in fact been a failure, with little or no damage inflicted on the enemy. And any damage done at Eindhoven, although unknown, would have been minimal.

Early the next day, I./KG 51 reported to Schenck that it had sent 19 aircraft to Giebelstadt as a new base of operations, but one had crashed near Köln. Fourteen machines were at Hopsten, of which just three were serviceable, while four more were at Rheine, two of which were serviceable. Another jet was serviceable at Münster, as was one at Oldenburg-Klausheide. There were four unserviceable aircraft at Hesepe. The *Geschwader* advised that it was suffering from a lack of priming fuel on the airfields in its area.

Heinrich Haeffner was in the air again early in the afternoon when I. *Gruppe* attacked targets in the Hagenau Forest and around Alsace. Later, he took off for a second mission. Haeffner recalled;

'The *Schwarm* leader approached the target from above the cloud at 9000 m. Our flight time to the target appeared unusually long to me. When we finally dropped through the clouds I was able to recognise Remiremont [126 km southwest of Hagenau]. Our leader was hopelessly lost! We dropped our bombs there and quickly turned for home.'

However, Haeffner's fuel ran low, and in restarting one of his engines, which he had earlier switched off for reasons of fuel economy, it caught fire so he had to put down in a field next to the runway.

During the evening of 2 January 5. *Jagddivision* enquired of KG 51 why it had not attacked the targets requested by *Heeresgruppe* H (Army Group H). The unit responded that small area attacks were not possible without knowledge of the terrain. Furthermore, the *Geschwader* complained about receiving target information late.

On the 3rd, I./KG 51 reported a strength of 21 aircraft, of which 18 were serviceable. I. *Gruppe* reported that 'all aircraft of II./KG 51 are in the stocks of I./KG 51'. Four Me 262s were at Schwäbisch Hall and four at Lechfeld. These aircraft were probably reserve machines left behind by II. *Gruppe* when it became operational. The unit is believed to have flown 16 sorties during the course of the day, including one in which Leutnant Batel took off from Giebelstadt to attack enemy troop concentrations. Having dropped his ordnance on target, Batel returned safely to base.

From Allied monitoring of German radio traffic, there is evidence to suggest that KG 51 was deployed on at least one occasion on 8 January to 'attack' an enemy bomber formation in order to force it to jettison its bombs, but the unit was ordered not to 'accept combat'.

That day, I./KG 51 reported that it had 32 aircraft on strength,

An Me 262A-2a of 2./KG 51 in typical scribble pattern camouflage receives an electrics and hydraulics test while supported by tripod trestles at a snow-covered airfield. The lack of national markings suggests a recent paint overspray. The aircraft is fitted with ETC 503 bomb racks, and its nose and tail fin tip have had the *Staffel* colour of red applied

including six that had only recently arrived. Just two days later the *Generalquartiermeister* reported no fewer than 52 Me 262s in total on the strength of I. and II./KG 51. On the 10th, the strength of I./KG 51 was 28 aircraft, four being off strength due to damage. It was further reported that all the jets in 1./KG 51 were A-1as fitted with four 30 mm cannon, and that most jets in 2. and 3. *Staffeln* were similarly armed.

Despite the poor weather on 10 January, 12 Me 262s from I./KG 51 supported a German ground assault around Hagenau in Alsace/Lorraine. Leutnant Batel is believed to have shot down a P-47 of the 324th FG southwest of Lauterbourg, but this victory was offset by the 80 percent damage inflicted to the Me 262A-2a of 2./KG 51's Oberleutnant von Ritter-Rittershain when it landed at Giebelstadt, and the crash-landing of Oberleutnant Gustav Stephan of 3./KG 51 following hits by enemy ground fire northwest of Münster.

Oberleutnant Heinz Strothmann of 2. *Staffel* attempted to land on one engine at Giebelstadt, but the nosewheel of his Messerschmitt failed to extend. He tried to go around again, but this was impossible with the undercarriage and landing flaps extended. At about 30 m, one wing dropped and the aircraft dived into the ground and immediately burst into flames. On reaching the crash site, Strothmann's comrades were astonished to find that he had suffered only shock, minor bruises and burns, and had a bad cut to the back of his head. Another aircraft, flown by Oberfeldwebel Wiese of 3./KG 51, was not so lucky, being shot down after takeoff 16 km west of Giebelstadt. The pilot was killed.

The targets for I./KG 51 on 13 January were enemy troop concentrations in the Hagenauer Forest. The *Gruppe* was in the air during the early afternoon, its aircraft conducting bombing and cannon-strafing attacks. But four Me 262s were lost, including the jet flown by Unteroffizier Alfred Färber of 1./KG 51. He fell victim to 55th FG Mustang pilot Lt Walter J Konantz, who, as he circled Giebelstadt airfield, 'caught him easily as he was in a medium turn, and I got a long burst into him from 200 yards. He caught fire near the port jet unit and made a diving turn straight into the ground about half-a-mile from the aerodrome. He exploded with a big flash of flame when he hit'.

The next morning at 0841 hrs, Haeffner, Wieczorek and Batel took off to attack targets near Durrenbach. Their Me 262A-2as were each loaded with a pair of 250 kg bombs and drop tanks. Despite light flak and the presence of enemy fighters in the target area, the Me 262s dropped their ordnance on American tank columns, with hits being observed. However, two Me 262s were also lost on this day. One, piloted by Unteroffizier Friedrich Christoph of 6./KG 51, was shot down as it landed at Rheine by a Spitfire IX of No 332 (Norwegian) Sqn, and the other, flown by Oswald von Ritter-Rittershain, was destroyed by flak at Surbourg, near Detweiler, while on a mission to attack enemy troop assemblies. Both pilots were killed.

Meanwhile, Hauptmann Karl-Heinz Wilke had been appointed *Kommandeur* of NAG 1, intended as a new Me 262 reconnaissance *Gruppe*. A few days later, Oberleutnant Wilhelm Knoll was made *Kapitän* of 1. *Staffel*, which was to be formed from elements of 1./F 121. However, the equipping process proved to be extremely slow. By 19 January, the *Gruppe* reported just two pilots and no aircraft on strength. The *Stab*,

Oberleutnant Heinz Strothmann of 2./KG 51, photographed in the cockpit of an Me 262. He survived a dramatic crash-landing at Giebelstadt on 10 January 1945 but was subsequently killed in a crash while landing at Saaz in early May

Debate exists as to the identity of this aircraft, but it may well be Me 262A-1a/U3 Wk-Nr. 170111, seen at Schwäbisch Hall or Lechfeld on 1 January 1945. It is believed that the portside engine failed shortly after takeoff while the aircraft was being piloted by Oberleutnant Herward Braunegg of *Kommando Panther*. He is possibly the pilot seen climbing onto the wing. The aircraft was about to undertake a reconnaissance mission, but Braunegg was forced to return. During a high-speed landing the nosewheel collapsed, the Me 262 suffering five percent damage

Another view of the Me 262A-1a/U3 (believed to have been Wk-Nr. 170111) seen at Schwäbisch Hall or Lechfeld in early 1945 following a crash-landing while being flown by Oberleutnant Herward Braunegg of *Kommando Panther*. This photograph shows the two Rb 50/30 cameras installed in what would usually be the gun housing. The barrel of the aircraft's repositioned single 30 MK 108 cannon can be seen in the nose

1. and 2./NAG 1 were at Herzogenaurach, and after a few days the *Stab* had a solitary Me 262 and four Bf 110s on strength, but the two *Staffeln* were still without aircraft or pilots.

Eventually, around ten pilots assembled at Herzogenaurach for familiarisation on the jet. They were quickly sent on a high-altitude adjustment course conducted at a remote ski hut on the *Zugspitze*. This was followed by a week of theoretical instruction on the construction and functioning of jet engines at Schwabstadtl. Finally, at

Laden with groundcrew, a semi-tracked *Kettenkrad* tractor pulls Me 262A-1a/U3 Wk-Nr. 500259 'White 3' of III./EJG 2 away from its dispersal at Lechfeld in the spring of 1945. This jet was eventually handed over to 1./NAG 6, where it was flown by Oberleutnant Georg Keck and Unteroffizier Heinz Huxold on photo-reconnaissance missions

Major Friedrich Heinz Schultze, a veteran of the North African campaigns led NAG 6 from 20 January 1945. His Me 262s would supply vital information to German army commanders on the Western Front in their final defensive battles of 1945

the beginning of February, practical instruction commenced at Lechfeld. This would last six weeks, and included takeoffs, circuits, high-altitude flights, ferry flights, formation flying, blind-flying and RATO starts. By 17 January, *Stab*/NAG 1 reported two jets on strength.

Kommando Panther, operating under 5. *Jagddivision* control, flew reconnaissance missions over the Hagenau-Strassburg area during mid-January. On the 20th, Braunegg's *Kommando* was incorporated into 2./NAG 6, with Braunegg taking over command. Major Friedrich Heinz Schultze, from the staff of the *General der Aufklärer*, took overall command of the *Gruppe* from Major Hermann Harbig, while Oberleutnant Georg Keck was *Kapitän* of 1./NAG 6. Schultze held a keen interest in the possibilities offered by high-speed, jet-powered reconnaissance aircraft, and had studied the reports of the experiences of the Ar 234-equipped *Kommando Götz*, as well as the periodic reports from Braunegg, which had been prepared for his immediate superior, Generalmajor von Barsewisch.

KG 51 launched a major effort from Giebelstadt on 23 January when targets in France were attacked. Leutnante Hubert Lange and Heid of 1. and 2. *Staffel*, respectively, were airborne during the morning. Heid ran into ten enemy fighters and also encountered flak, taking hits to his jet, but he returned home safely having struck his assigned target 188 km southwest of his base. Lange also experienced flak, but managed to drop his bombs from 1600 m and returned to Giebelstadt. Wilhelm Kröfges and Wilhelm Batel also took off to attack the enemy during the morning.

Heid took off for a second mission in the early afternoon accompanied by Kröfges, but he was forced to return with a technical problem to his starboard Jumo engine. Hauptmann Karl-Heinz Bührig of 3./KG 51 was operational over a target at Gries, in France, during the afternoon. His Me 262A-2a was hit by ground fire but he was able to return.

Flt Lts F L McLeod and R V Dennis, flying Tempests from No 56 Sqn, claimed an Me 262 shot down on 23 January, and it is believed that their victim was the bomb-laden aircraft of Unteroffizier Kubizek from 4./KG 51, who was shot down near Paderborn. Kubizek bailed out and came down in a tree, from which he was left hanging for some time.

On the 29th Heinrich Haeffner flew an eventful mission;

'I took off alone at 1122 hrs on a meteorological reconnaissance flight – I was also ordered to attack targets near Colmar. Immediately after takeoff, I climbed through clouds and approached my target from a height of 10,000 m. There were only scattered clouds west of the Rhine, and I quickly found Colmar. Descending to 5000 m, I could clearly see enemy tanks and troops. I kept an eye on the tanks, keeping them in my bombsight despite the heavy flak. I released both my bombs from this altitude and then steeply climbed away. Moments later there was a loud bang, and my aircraft began to rotate during the climb. The left turbine had stopped and the engine cowlings had burst open. It looked as though I had been hit by flak.

'By this time I had reached the Schwarzwald on the east bank of the Rhine, still above the clouds. At first I wanted to bail out, but then I realised that I could still maintain level flight with one wing down. The compass was behaving erratically, so I had to rely on my little armband compass. Seeing that I was able to keep flying, I requested Y-guidance to Giebelstadt. On being told "descend, railway station under you", I knew I could now dive through the clouds since the airfield was below me.

'With a dead port engine, I descended carefully through clouds until I could see the ground. Unfortunately there was no airfield to be seen, there was no Würzburg and no River Main. My fuel gauges were approaching zero, so I radioed ground control, telling them that I was "very thirsty" and needed an emergency landing field. Ground control now told me that I was ten kilometres east of Kitzingen airfield. I requested the bearing of the runway so as to avoid having to fly turns over the airfield. The answer was "270 degrees", and I was therefore able to make a direct approach, dropping the undercarriage and landing flaps with compressed air. All pipes and cables were damaged and the undercarriage would not lock down, however. I readied myself for a belly-landing and put my Messerschmitt into deep snow in an east-west direction. The undercarriage collapsed immediately, and I skidded through the snow, only coming to a stop directly in front of a hangar.'

In the afternoon I./KG 51 was briefed to attack Illhaeusern, 37 km northwest of Freiburg-im-Breisgau. Leutnant Lange's Me 262A-1a, fitted with a single SC 250 under the fuselage, received flak damage over the target area. He dropped his bomb from 1200 m and saw it explode within the town. Leutnant Heid carried a pair of SD 250s, and he dropped them on the target with good effect. On his return to Giebelstadt, however, he ran out of fuel and was forced to make an emergency landing seven kilometres short of the airfield.

As January 1945 drew to a close, Oberstleutnant Schenck handed command of KG 51 to Oberstleutnant Rudolf Hallensleben and took up the appointment of *Inspizient für Strahlflugzeuge* (Inspector of Jet Aircraft) in the RLM. At the end of the month I./KG 51 had about 50 Me 262s operational, II./KG 51 had 23 and *Kommando Braunegg*/2./NAG 6 had five. Worryingly, however, attrition due to combat and non-combat casualties was taking its toll – the total strength of I. and II./KG 51 at the end of January 1945 was equal to the strength of I. *Gruppe* alone at the end of November 1944.

Throughout January, a small ad hoc unit had been at work assessing the Me 262 in pure ground-attack terms (as opposed to bombing). That month, the *General der Schlachtflieger*, newly promoted Generalmajor Hubertus Hitschhold, assigned experienced Stuka pilot Major Heinrich Brücker (a former *Kommodore* of SG 4, but latterly serving on the staff of the military science department of the Luftwaffe General Staff) to head up the *Erprobungsschwarm Me 262 des General der Schlachtflieger*. The task of this small unit, comprised of Brücker and three other pilots, was to assess the Me 262 in the pure ground-attack role with bombs and cannon. The unit commenced its activites in late January at Neuburg with Me 262s taken on from 15./EKG 1.

Oberstleutnant Rudolf Hallensleben took over command of KG 51 from Wolfgang Schenck on 1 February 1945. From January 1943 Hallensleben had led KG 76 over Tunisia, the Mediterranean, Sicily, Italy (where this photograph was taken) and then during the bombing campaign against the British Isles in early 1944. Subsequently briefly serving as *Kommodore* of KG 2, Hallensleben was awarded the Knight's Cross on 29 October 1943 after completing more than 200 combat missions

Moving north to join 2./KG 51 at Hopsten in late February, the jets conducted trial operations loaded with one 500 kg or two 250 kg bombs. It was found that shallow dive-bombing from about 4500 m or lower achieved the best results, with a lateral interval of about 90 m. Targets were approached until they disappeared from sight under either of the jet engine units, and then the pilot entered a dive at an angle of 30 degrees, using a standard Reflex sight for aiming. A speed of 850-900 km/h was attained, and further acceleration was prevented by pulling the nose up and reducing the speed of the engines to about 6000 rpm. Bombs were released at an altitude of about 900-1070 m.

Following early dive-bombing trials, pilots quickly realised that it was essential that they emptied the rear fuel tank before pulling out of the dive, or the Me 262 would become tail-heavy and nose up abruptly. This in turn could result in the wings being torn off. In fact, several pilots from KG 51 were known to have been lost this way.

Heinrich Brücker also conducted ground-strafing operations against Allied troops and vehicles in the Me 262, and he destroyed several trucks in the process. However, he told Allied interrogators after the war that he did not view the Me 262 as being a particularly good platform for strafing because the 30 mm MK 108 cannon had so low a muzzle velocity that an attack had to take place at an altitude of 400 m or less to ensure accuracy. Furthermore, the 360 rounds of ammunition carried by the Me 262 was too small for the amount of target area that could be covered by the high-speed aircraft. Brücker also felt that there was insufficient armour to protect a pilot from flak.

In late January 1945 three Me 262s were delivered to NAG 6 and a trio of new pilots (Leutnante Hellmut Tetzner, Herbert Schubert and Christian Haber) posted in. Schubert was quickly sent into the air, accompanied by Oberleutnant Engelhart, to fly a reconnaissance mission over the Vosges on 1 February. Flying at an altitude of 4000 m, the pilots were surprised by the sight of a V2 rocket as it suddenly shot up through the sky just 500 metres away from their jets!

In early February the Allies prepared to drive on the Rhine. Their advance would be over a front of 400 km from the Swiss border, across eastern France, Luxembourg, Belgium and into Holland. In the north, the forces of Bradley and Montgomery would mount a series of assaults on the great river and attempt exploitation of the German defences. The commander of the 82nd Airborne Division noted in his diary on 3 February, 'The Germans appear to be beaten, and beaten badly'.

Yet, the day before, no fewer than 25 Me 262s from I./KG 51 were detailed to attack troops of the French First Army in the Colmar area, east of the Vosges, in support of 19. *Armee*. The *Gruppe* reported

A pilot assists groundcrew loading a pair of SC 500 bombs onto the *Wikingerschiff* bomb racks of Me 262A-2a Wk-Nr. 111603 on a snow-covered airfield in the winter of 1944/45. The armourers are using a hydraulic trolley. This aircraft performed bomb-dropping tests in January 1945, before being transferred to I./KG 51 the following month

Leutnant Hellmut Tetzner of 2./NAG 6

22 aircraft over the target and explosions at Ostheim, north of Colmar, together with hits on vehicle concentrations on the northern edge of the Colmar Forest. Hubert Lange of 1./KG 51 was assigned the railway station at Ostheim as a target, but as he approached it he was fired upon by flak batteries. Nevertheless, he was able to carry out a gliding attack and drop his bomb from 1600 m, observing it hit the area between the station and the town. Lange then safely returned to Giebelstadt.

Once again, Heinrich Haeffner was flying;

'I was allocated a new Me 262, and took off to attack Colmar at 1321 hrs. Approaching the target, I again met a large number of enemy bomber formations with strong fighter escort heading for the Reich. As on earlier occasions, I flew towards the fighters and fired several bursts at them. The fighters immediately jettisoned their tanks, expecting an attack. I climbed away steeply, the fighters being unable to follow. Having dropped my bombs on Colmar, I touched down at Giebelstadt at 1420 hrs. The groundcrew quickly refuelled my aircraft and rearmed it with bombs.'

One jet, however – an Me 262A-1a from 3./KG 51 – was lost five kilometres west of Giebelstadt due to an engine fire, and its pilot, Hauptmann Bührig, was killed.

Me 262s of 5./KG 51 flew operations against a supply dump at Maastricht, 900 m north of the railway bridge, on 3 February. This was, however, viewed as an 'alternative target'. On the 4th, a single jet from KG 51 dropped two SC 250 bombs in the Barr area, north of Schlettstadt, during a weather reconnaissance flight, but results were not observed. Next day, 3. *Jagddivision* instructed that KG 51 was to be used in ways 'which are decisive and promise success' – perhaps an indication that recent results were not viewed as being entirely acceptable.

On 8 February, 20 Me 262s were sent aloft to attack enemy troop movements in the Colmar-Mulhouse area. Eighteen made it to the target, with two having to break off due to technical difficulties. No results were observed, but no losses were suffered. Three aircraft from II./KG 51 were damaged, however, due to accidents. Two crashed at Essen-Mühlheim and one, flown by Feldwebel Hans Trenke of 6./KG 51, was shot at by German flak and suffered 20 percent damage.

The veritable Heinrich Haeffner of 2./KG 51 was also operational this day;

'At 0920 hrs I took off in very bad weather for a weather reconnaissance mission and a possible bombing attack on Neu-Breisach. By the time of my approach the weather was so bad that I wanted to break off the mission. West of the Rhine, however, the cloud cover had lifted enough for me to attack a bridge near Neu-Breisach. During the afternoon I flew another mission with Hauptmann Abrahamczik to Colmar. After our bomb attack, we engaged three bomber boxes on our return flight. We had seen them on our flight to Colmar. They were escorted by approximately 20 fighters. We fired a few cannon salvos and the enemy drop tanks then rained down to earth. We flew quickly to Giebelstadt, as we still had a long distance to cover. We landed at Giebelstadt at 1550 hrs.'

The Me 262 reconnaissance force was also active at this time, with NAG 6 being ordered to transfer to Münster-Handorf and

Leutnant Herbert Schubert of 2./NAG 6

Essen-Mühlheim for operations over the Western Front. Three Me 262s from 2./NAG 6 (formerly *Kommando Panther*) flew photo-reconnaissance sorties in the Roermond area, where the British Second Army was engaged against forces of the German *Heeresgruppe* H, as well as to the west of the Scheldt, but all were unsuccessful owing to the bad weather. Another two jets from NAG 6 flew road reconnaissance in the Strassburg-Schlettstadt-Colmar area, but again this was only partially successful due to the weather.

On 10 February 2./NAG 6 despatched two Me 262s on a photo-reconnaissance mission in the Zabern-Strassburg area, while KG 51 also sent one of its jets on a similar sortie over the same location.

At command-level, OKL instructed *Luftflotte Reich* that daylight operations by jet formations and night operations by night ground-attack units should be concentrated in the vicinity of the front between Nijmegen and Schleiden. As part of this instruction I./KG 51 transferred back to Hopsten from Giebelstadt, while II./KG 51 was at Rheine. In another initiative, during his daily conference *Reichsmarschall* Göring proposed that the *Geschwader Stab* of KG 51 and the Ar 234-equipped KG 76 be combined to form a single *Fliegerbrigade*, but this did not advance beyond the proposal stage.

By the 14th, British and Canadian forces were approaching the south bank of the Rhine opposite the fortified town of Kleve, leading KG 51 to fly a total of 55 sorties against Allied ground targets in the area during the day. Kleve lay between the Reichswald and a large flood plain close to the river, and in the advance path of the British XXX Corps. The terrain consisted of impenetrable forest – difficult for Allied tanks, with relatively few roads, and those that did exist were narrow, covered in snow and unsurfaced. A thaw had come early, causing considerable localised flooding, and the forces of *Heeresgruppe* H used all these factors as part of their defence.

Me 262s worked in cooperation with Ar 234s from KG 76 in an early morning strike on Kleve. The units reported 35 aircraft over the target between 0755 hrs and 0916 hrs, 13 of which came from KG 51. Four Me 262s made it as far as the target, while one broke off due to a technical

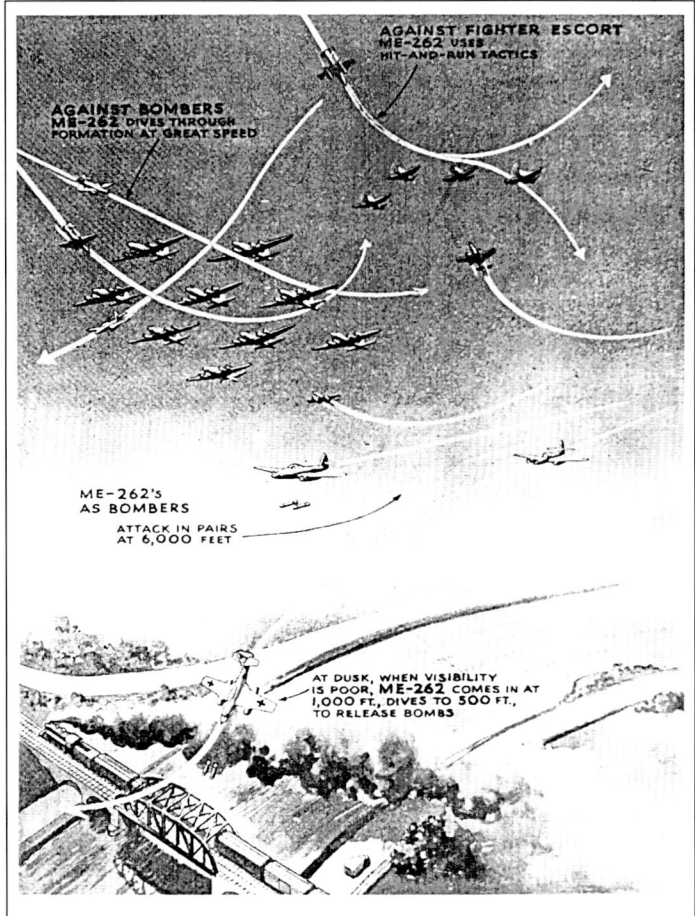

TRIPLE-THREAT TACTICS made the ME-262 a troublesome customer. Carrying at least four 30 millimeter cannons in its nose and two 551-pound bombs under its fuselage, it was adapted to low-level bombing and strafing of Allied installations behind the lines as well as to lightning strikes at our bomber formations. Its heavy armor—15 millimeters thick in some places—enabled it to tangle with our fighters if necessary. When carrying bombs, it was slowed down so much that it sometimes took along its own fighter escort. Allied troops called it "the silent strafer" because it streaked past with little sound.

'Troublesome customers' was how the USAAF viewed the Me 262s of KG 51 in a report from February 1945. There was a perceived 'triple threat' from the jets, which were able not only to strike at ground targets at dusk, but also to engage both enemy fighters and heavy bombers. This diagram from the February 1945 report illustrates that view

problem. 6./KG 51's Leutnant Dieter Mundt of dropped a single SD 250 from his jet on his assigned target at Zyfflich, northwest of Kranenburg (nine kilometres west of Kleve), having avoided an encounter with a formation of P-51s in the target area as well as heavy flak.

Mundt's *Staffelkamerad*, Unteroffizier Martin Golde, was briefed to attack troop assembly points in the same area, but instead he struck at Nijmegen as an alternative target, making a glide attack from a height of 2000 m. Golde landed safely at Essen-Mühlheim after a 29-minute sortie, whereupon his aircraft was rearmed and refuelled in readiness for a second mission, this time to Kranenburg. As he neared the target Golde spotted some Tempests, so he turned for the secondary target at Nijmegen, which he attacked in a glide from 1500 m. Golde returned to Essen 33 minutes later.

Also in the air for a second mission was Leutnant Mundt, who bombed Malden (seven kilometres south of Nijmegen) with a pair of SC 250s without interference. However, when fellow 6. *Staffel* pilot Leutnant Adolf Svoboda attempted to bomb Gennep (18 km southeast of Nijmegen), he encountered heavy flak, before four Spitfires attacked him. Despite this, Svoboda was able to drop his ordnance, but he noticed that it did not detonate.

Altogether, six jets landed at alternative airfields after the mission, but two Me 262A-2as and their pilots were reported missing. These unfortunates had been spotted by Typhoon pilots of No 439 Sqn RCAF, who were reforming after conducting an armed reconnaissance in the Coesfeld-Enschede area. Subsequently, Flt Lt Lyall C Shaver and ace Flg Off Hugh Fraser claimed two Me 262s destroyed after bouncing the jets. Both Oberleutnant Hans Georg Richter and Feldwebel Werner Witzmann of 5./KG 51 died when their jets crashed near Osterwick.

At Essen-Mühlheim, two aircraft of II. *Gruppe* were damaged in crash-landings. A further operation, also mounted with KG 76, took place between 1600 hrs and 1720 hrs when two aircraft attacked Nijmegen as an alternative target, the observation of effects being hindered by bad weather. Five jets were forced to break off the mission because of technical difficulties, while four more from I. and II./KG 51 were damaged in these attacks.

Heinrich Haeffner recounted the pressures now being felt by the *Geschwader*;

'At 1650 hrs [on 14 February] I took off for an attack on Kleve, accompanied by Hauptmann Abrahamczik and Oberfeldwebel Wieczorek. I was ordered to land back at Rheine after the mission so as to assume operational command of 5./KG 51. However, things were to turn out quite differently. Just before takeoff, ground control reported "Indians" (enemy fighters at great height) and "Sharks" (fighters at low level), but I didn't take notice of their exact position. Some 30 Bf 109s from JG 27 were over the field when we took off, their job being to protect us from the enemy fighters.

Personnel of NAG 6 outside their earth dug-out communications post possibly at Essen-Mühlheim in the spring of 1945

'Taking off as No 3, I was puzzled to see Hauptmann Abrahamczik break sharply to the left, while Oberfeldwebel Wieczorek turned left too. Lifting off, I pressed the undercarriage retraction switch and saw tracers crossing ahead of me. Then bullets crashed into my aircraft, big holes appearing in the wings – a Tempest flashed past. I pushed my Messerschmitt down to ground level, but was unable to gain speed. My aircraft had full tanks and carried two 250 kg bombs and ammunition. In the rear view mirror I saw another Tempest coming in for the attack. It shot at my right turbine, which immediately stopped.

'On one engine, I flew very low towards Rheine, hoping that our flak would scare the Tempests off. After a third attack, the extra fuel tank caught fire and the left engine began losing power. The cockpit then started to fill with smoke, so I pulled up sharply and jettisoned the canopy. Since the jet might crash at any moment, I undid my seat harness and pulled the microphone plug and oxygen hose from their sockets.

'At about 350 m, the aircraft dived over on to its starboard wing. I immediately bailed out and pulled the rip cord without counting the usual "21, 22, 23". It came as a shock when the rip cord handle came loose in my hand – something was seriously wrong. It was my first jump. Almost immediately I felt the gentle shock as the parachute opened safely. It was not fully deployed when I landed in a soft field close to a flak position near Rheine. From here I was able to telephone my headquarters, and was soon in a motor car back to Hopsten.'

Such events illustrated that when bombed-up, the Me 262 was slowed sufficiently for it to be caught by conventional fighters.

In a dusk operation at around 1700 hrs, Feldwebel Rudolf Hofmann of 3./KG 51 was shot down in his Me 262A-2a by a Spitfire. His jet dived straight into the ground and was destroyed. 14 February had been a black day for KG 51.

On the 15th *Luftflotte Reich* was directed by an order from *Reichsmarschall* Göring that I. and II./KG 51 and KG 76 (equipped

Me 262A-2a Wk-Nr. 111603 of I./KG 51, 'bombed up' with two SC 500s suspended from *Wikingerschiff* bomb racks on a snow-covered runway in late 1944 or early 1945

with four operational *Staffeln* of Ar 234s) were to be combined into one unit, known as a *Gefechtsverband* (Combat Group), under the command of the *Geschwader Kommodore* of KG 76, Oberstleutnant Robert Kowalewski.

Meanwhile, the reconnaissance units were active. On the 14th an advanced detachment of 1./NAG 6 arrived at Essen-Mühlheim and two of its jets flew photo-reconnaissance missions, one in the Drusenheim-Hagenau-Saarunion-Saarburg-Wassenheim area and the other over the Hagenau-Bischweiler-Brumath-Strassburg-Erstein area and west of the Rhine at Plosheim. Unteroffizier Heinz Huxold also flew a reconnaissance mission over Dresden, recording nothing but the destruction of a once beautiful city. Huxold did, however, have the satisfaction of apparently shooting down a P-51.

Next day, NAG 6 mounted four operations – two jets were sent on a reconnaissance mission to Zabern-Saarburg-Ingweiler, while another conducted reconnaissance west of the Rhine. Two more Me 262s flew 'road patrols' over the Zabern-St Avold-Ingweiler area, and a single aircraft performed an armed reconnaissance to the Hagenau-Zabern-Strassburg area.

Around ten pilots were sent to Lechfeld for reconnaissance training at this time too, but they did not carry out the high-altitude syllabus on the *Zugspitze* or the theoretical training at Schwabstadtl as the first cadre of pilots had done.

Operations continued on both the 16th and 17th, an Me 262 from NAG 6 flying a photo-reconnaissance sortie in the Strassburg-Habern-Ingweiler-Hagenau-Drusenheim area on the first day, while another jet covered Drusenheim-Hagenau-Saarunion-Salzbergen-Zabern-Strassburg on the 17th, but was forced to break off due to bad weather.

On 20 February 1./NAG 6 reported the loss of a reconnaissance aircraft, which was described in a report as an 'Me 262A-4'. This, it will be remembered, was a proposed production reconnaissance version of the Me 262. On the 21st Oberleutnant Knoll, *Staffelkapitän* of 1./NAG 1, who was converting to the jet, was killed when his Me 262A-1a/U3 crashed southwest of Landsberg-am-Lech. He had been on a familiarisation ferry flight when, southeast of Landsberg, he noticed a pair of P-51s. Using his speed advantage, he climbed to the same height as the American fighters and manoeuvred in behind them. Just before Knoll got into a position to open fire, the P-51s broke to the left and right, quickly turned behind him and shot the jet down. Following the death of Knoll, Hauptmann Dünkel was appointed as the new commander of 1./NAG 1.

Things were not much better for KG 51, as II. *Gruppe* lost four aircraft on the 21st – one crashed due to technical failure, one ran out of fuel near Aschendorf, one (piloted by Oberfähnrich Rohde) went missing and another failed to take off at Essen-Mühlheim for unknown reasons and suffered damage. However, seven of the *Gruppe's* jets did manage to fly nuisance attacks on troop concentrations in the Bedburg area, southeast of Kleve, throughout the day. Thirty-eight aircraft were reported over the target area between 1103 hrs and 1728 hrs. Ten jets broke off their attacks owing to technical difficulties, but no losses were suffered. Thirteen Me 262s from I./KG 51 targeted Allied troop

Unteroffizier Heinz Huxold of 1./NAG 6

With its distinctive bulged camera fairing, Me 262A-1a/U3 Wk-Nr. 500259 'White 3' of III./EJG 2 and later NAG 6 is towed across the concrete apron at Lechfeld in early 1945

Lt Oliven C Cowan of the USAAF's 365th FG watches from the cockpit of his P-47 Thunderbolt as his chief mechanic carefully paints an Me 262 'kill' marking onto the fighter. It marked Cowan's shooting down of Leutnant Kurt Piehl of 2./KG 51 on 22 February 1945

concentrations in the Kleve and Kessel areas between 1701 hrs and 1753 hrs, with one aircraft being slightly damaged.

Over the Western Front on 22 February, 19 Me 262s from KG 51 attacked US troop concentrations in the Inden, Aldenoven and Geilenkirchen areas between 1143 hrs and 1747 hrs. Towards the end of these attacks, at 1740 hrs, P-47s from the 365th FG were on patrol in the area when they were alerted to the presence of Me 262s. Lt Thomas N Threlkeld was flying as wingman to Lt Oliven C Cowan of the 388th FS, and he reported;

'I was flying "Elwood White Two" position when our squadron encountered Me 262s strafing on the deck. One of them tried to climb through us but was turned back down by "Red Flight". At this time I was on Lt Cowan's wing at about 11,000 ft. We went into a dive, and with the altitude advantage and a little water injection, my leader pulled up on his tail and fired a burst from his guns. The jet nosed down and struck the ground. There was a black puff of smoke and tiny pieces of wreckage when I passed over the spot.'

The Me 262, which was flown by Leutnant Kurt Piehl of 2./KG 51, crashed into the ground northwest of Düren.

On 23 February the US First and Ninth Armies began a heavy attack along the Roer, especially in the Jülich area. Despite increasingly poor weather and intense enemy flak, eight Me 262s from KG 51 attacked tank concentrations in dives with SD 250s in this area between 1027 hrs and 1649 hrs. No losses were suffered during this operation, although a jet from I./KG 51 was damaged when it hit an object on landing.

An Me 262 from NAG 6 flew an armed reconnaissance in the Drusenheim-Hagenau-Ingweiler-Brumath area that same day, while another photographed the Rhine from Basel to Gambsheim.

Eight Me 262s offered cover to Ar 234s of KG 76 on the 24th and then attacked enemy concentrations in the Linnich-Düren area, sustaining only light combat damage. KG 51 suffered three losses from non-operational causes, however. In I. *Gruppe*, Feldwebel Horst Schulz crashed at Essen due to a technical failure, and in II. *Gruppe* an aircraft was damaged on takeoff and Oberfeldwebel Otto Zeppenfeld (of 5. *Staffel*) was lost at Rheine when his jet crashed due to technical defects. Finally,

An NCO technician hands down the film magazine of one of the Zeiss Rb 50/30 cameras to a mechanic. The jet is Me 262A-1a/U3 Wk-Nr. 500259 'White 3' of III./EJG 2 and later NAG 6, seen here at Lechfeld in early 1945

The film magazine from one of the Zeiss Rb 50/30 cameras fitted to Me 262A-1a/U3 Wk-Nr. 500259 'White 3' of III./EJG 2 is taken away for development following a reconnaissance mission. In this typical scene at Lechfeld, a *Kettenkrad* waits to tow the aircraft to its shelter. Note the tow bar lying on the ground at bottom left

fellow 5. *Staffel* pilot Unteroffizier Arthur Döhler had his machine badly shot up by fighter-bombers over Rheine.

After Düren was taken by American forces on 26 February, Thunderbolts of the 365th FG sighted 16 Me 262s of I./KG 51 near the town at 0840 hrs and, during the sporadic actions that followed, claimed several damaged. The 366th FG encountered jets on two separate sorties that same day – the first time, at 1020 hrs near Gladbach, resulted in claims for two Me 262s damaged. P-47s of the 405th FG met Messerschmitts east of Erkelen and claimed one damaged at 1040 hrs. Ten minutes later, P-47s from the 373rd FG engaged jets between Linnich and Jülich, again claiming one damaged. It is almost certain that most, if not all, the German aircraft came from KG 51. The Luftwaffe situation report stated;

'Twelve Me 262s from KG 51 and 20 Ar 234s from KG 76 attacked enemy targets in the Linnich area between 0812 hrs and 1634 hrs. Hits were observed on roads, bridges and towns – two aircraft, but no pilots, were lost. Eighteen Me 262s from KG 51 flew continuous attacks on Jülich between 0753 hrs and 1326 hrs. Hits were observed both on the town and the railway station, one pilot and one aircraft being posted missing.'

On the 26th, the OKL *Führungsstab* ordered NAG 1 to transfer from Herzogenaurach to Hennef, near Bonn, while 2./NAG 6 was to locate to Münster-Handorf. On the 28th, a solitary Me 262 from NAG 6 flew a photo-reconnaissance mission along roads in the Bischweiler-Ingweiler-Zabern-Strassburg area.

By the end of February 1945, all pilots of NAG 6 had been trained on the Me 262. Around 16-18 pilots were reported as being on strength, with four aircraft in the *Stab* and 16 in 1. *Staffel*. The draconian measures put into place by Hitler's 'plenipotentiaries' had helped to drastically 'increase' jet production in February, with no fewer than 13 Me 262s being converted into reconnaissance aircraft. All these went to NAG 6.

At the end of February the Headquarters of the RAF's 2nd TAF conceded that, 'There has been a noticeable increase in jet aircraft activity in the northern sector, and this is part explained by the transfer on the 13th of Me 262s of KG 51 to Mühlheim and Rheine'.

COLOUR PLATES

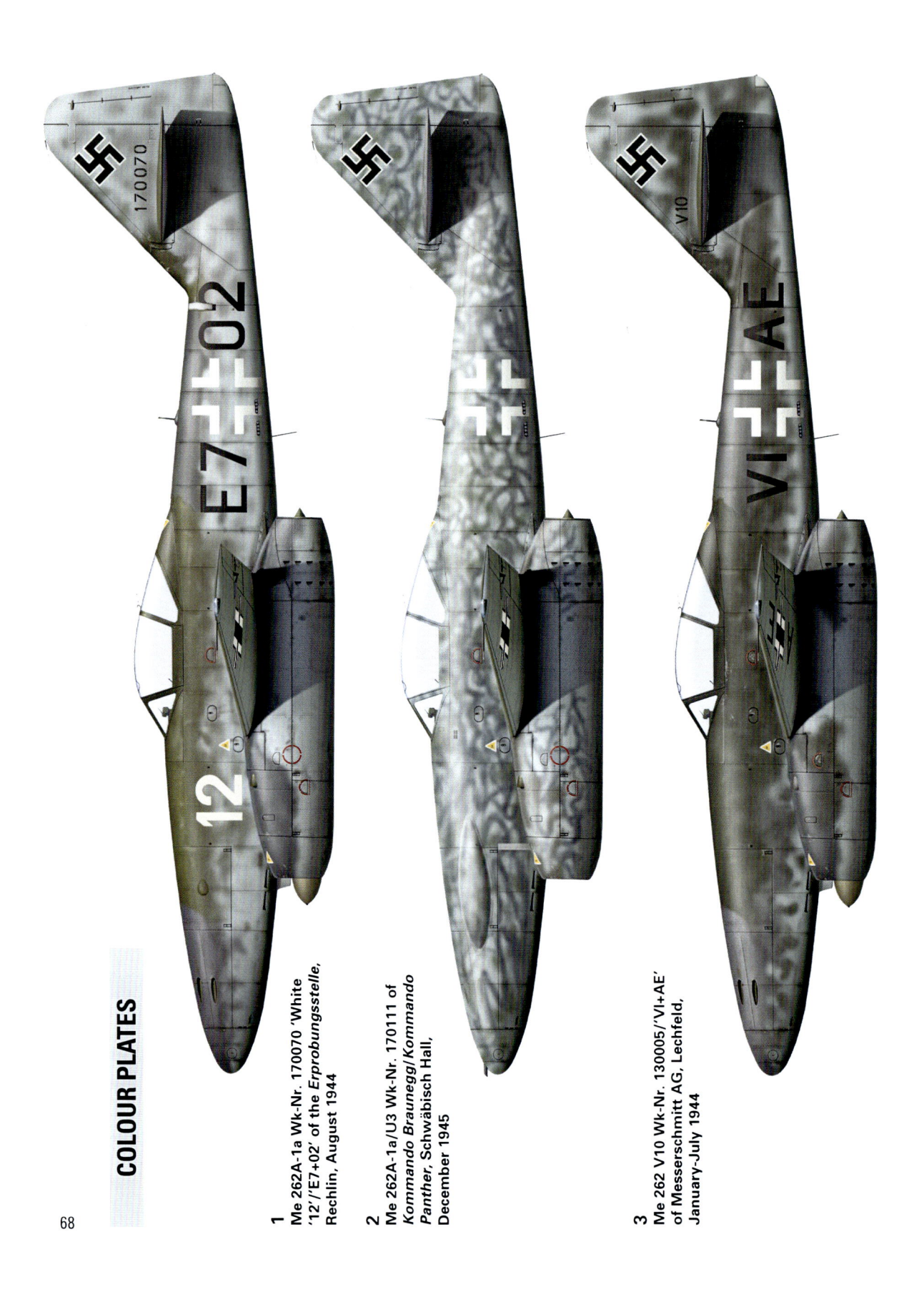

1
Me 262A-1a Wk-Nr. 170070 'White '12'/'E7+02' of the *Erprobungsstelle*, Rechlin, August 1944

2
Me 262A-1a/U3 Wk-Nr. 170111 of *Kommando Braunegg/Kommando Panther*, Schwäbisch Hall, December 1945

3
Me 262 V10 Wk-Nr. 130005/'VI+AE' of Messerschmitt AG, Lechfeld, January-July 1944

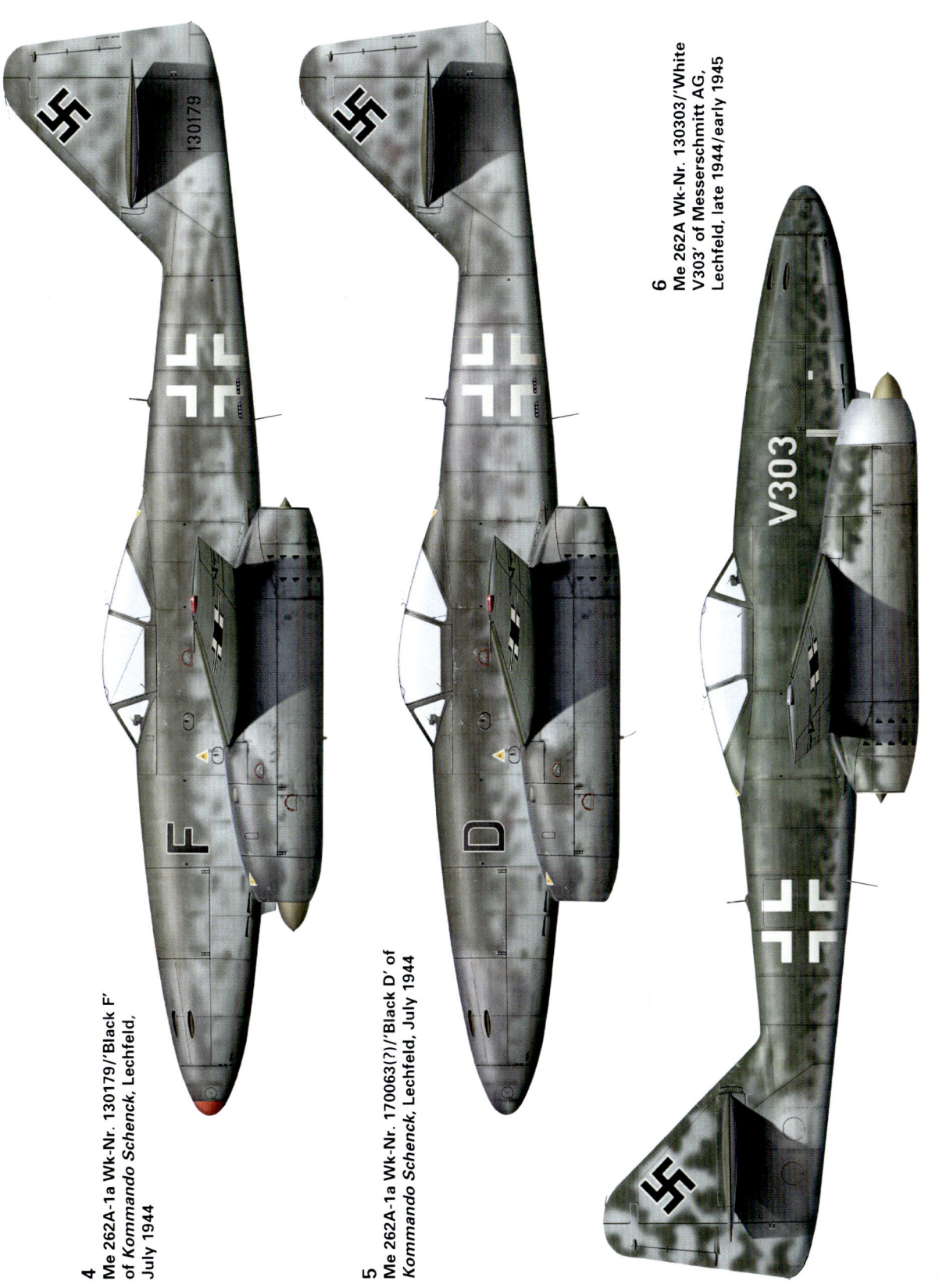

4
Me 262A-1a Wk-Nr. 130179/'Black F' of *Kommando Schenck*, Lechfeld, July 1944

5
Me 262A-1a Wk-Nr. 170063(?)/'Black D' of *Kommando Schenck*, Lechfeld, July 1944

6
Me 262A Wk-Nr. 130303/'White V303' of Messerschmitt AG, Lechfeld, late 1944/early 1945

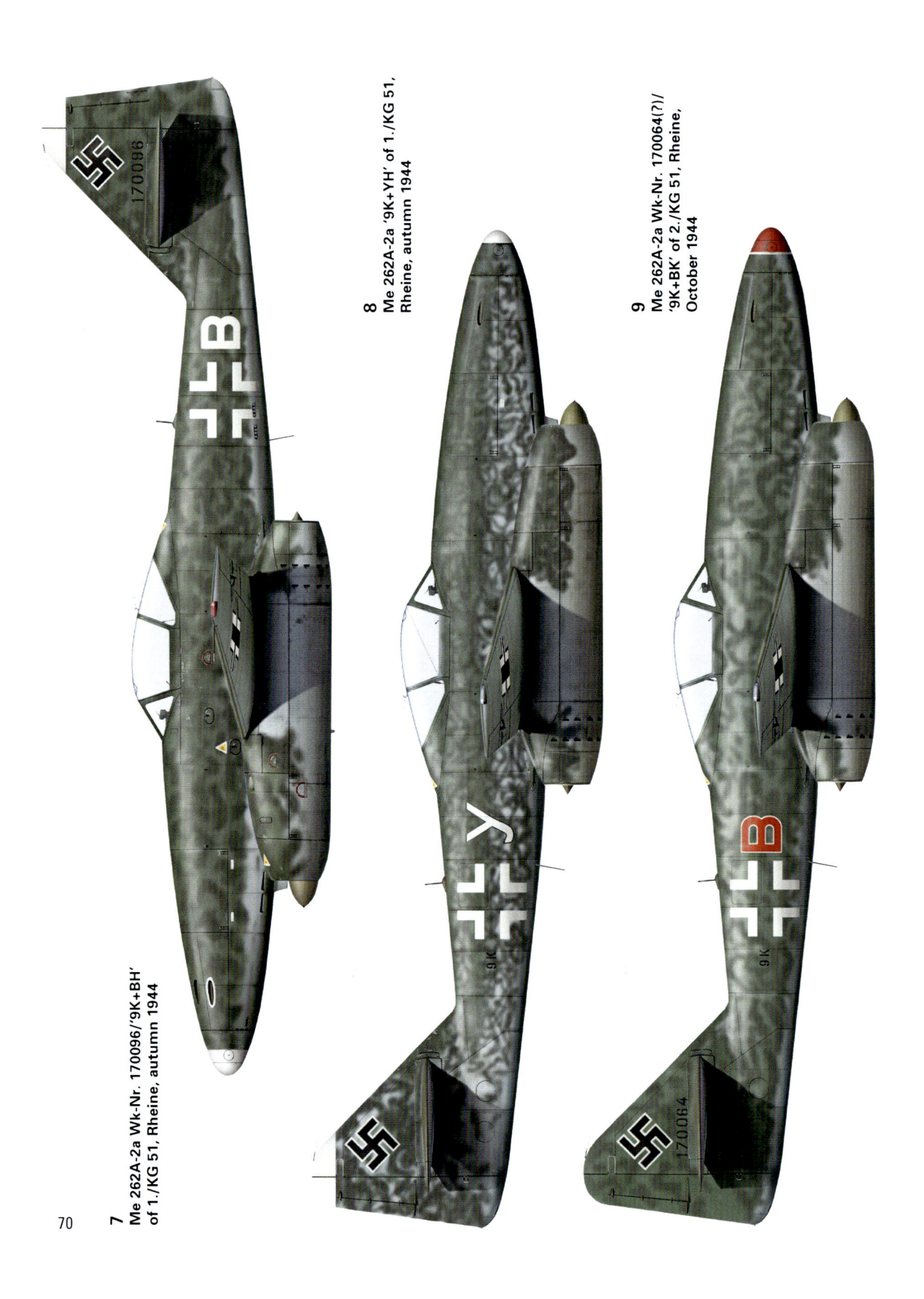

7
Me 262A-2a Wk-Nr. 170096/'9K+BH' of 1./KG 51, Rheine, autumn 1944

8
Me 262A-2a '9K+YH' of 1./KG 51, Rheine, autumn 1944

9
Me 262A-2a Wk-Nr. 170064(?)/ '9K+BK' of 2./KG 51, Rheine, October 1944

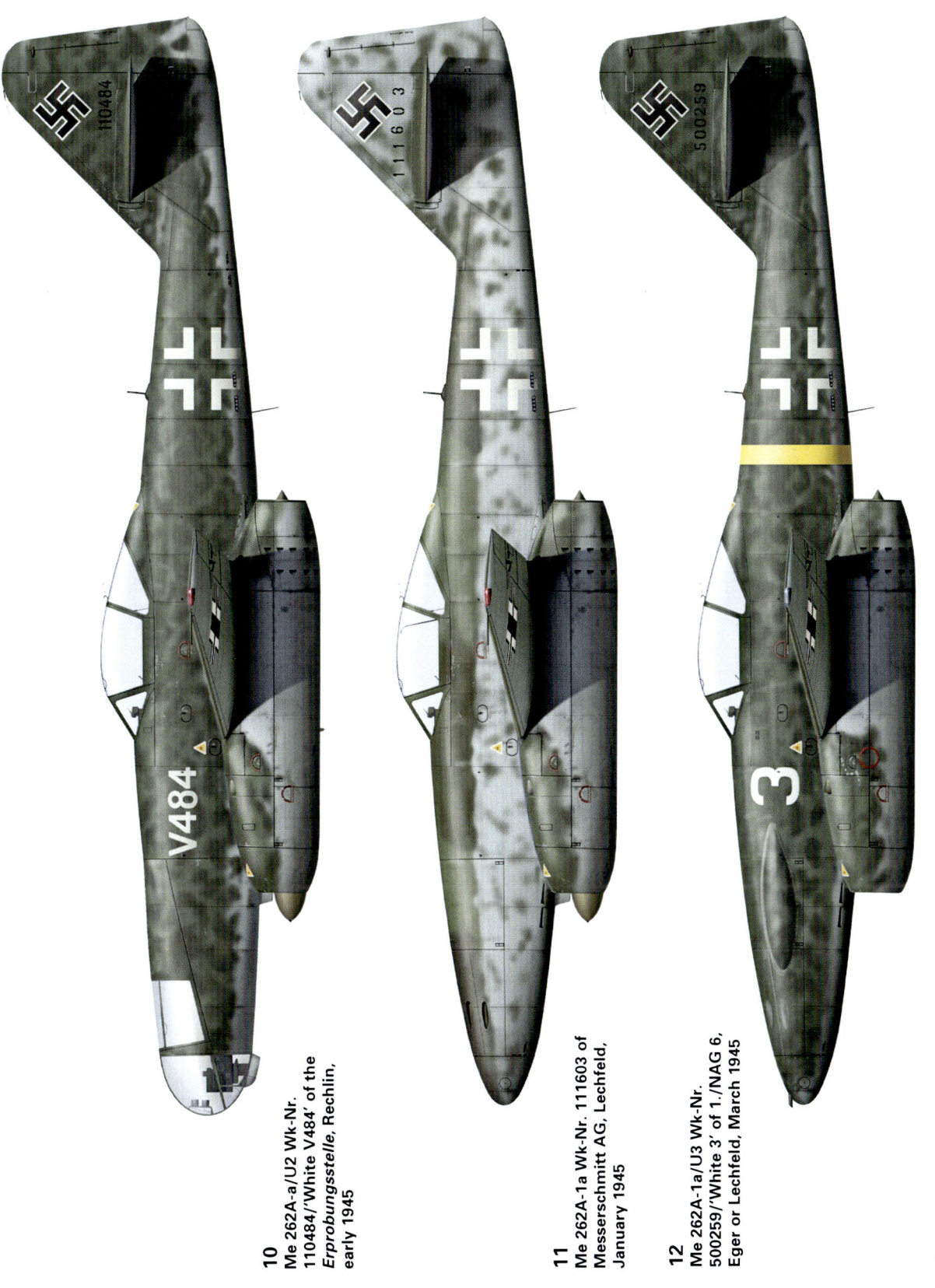

10
Me 262A-a/U2 Wk-Nr. 110484/'White V484' of the *Erprobungsstelle*, Rechlin, early 1945

11
Me 262A-1a Wk-Nr. 111603 of Messerschmitt AG, Lechfeld, January 1945

12
Me 262A-1a/U3 Wk-Nr. 500259/'White 3' of 1./NAG 6, Eger or Lechfeld, March 1945

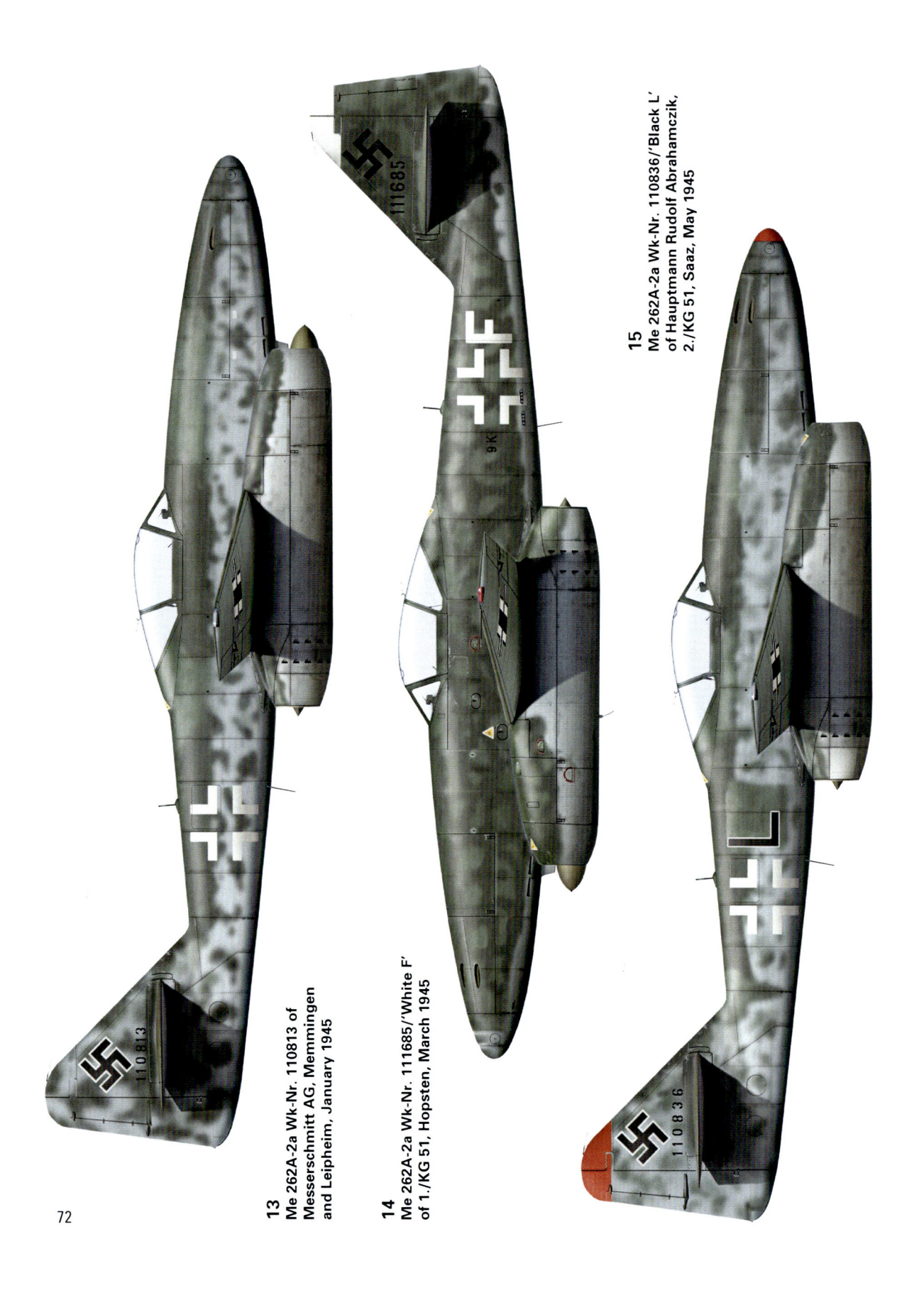

13
Me 262A-2a Wk-Nr. 110813 of Messerschmitt AG, Memmingen and Leipheim, January 1945

14
Me 262A-2a Wk-Nr. 111685/'White F' of 1./KG 51, Hopsten, March 1945

15
Me 262A-2a Wk-Nr. 110836/'Black L' of Hauptmann Rudolf Abrahamczik, 2./KG 51, Saaz, May 1945

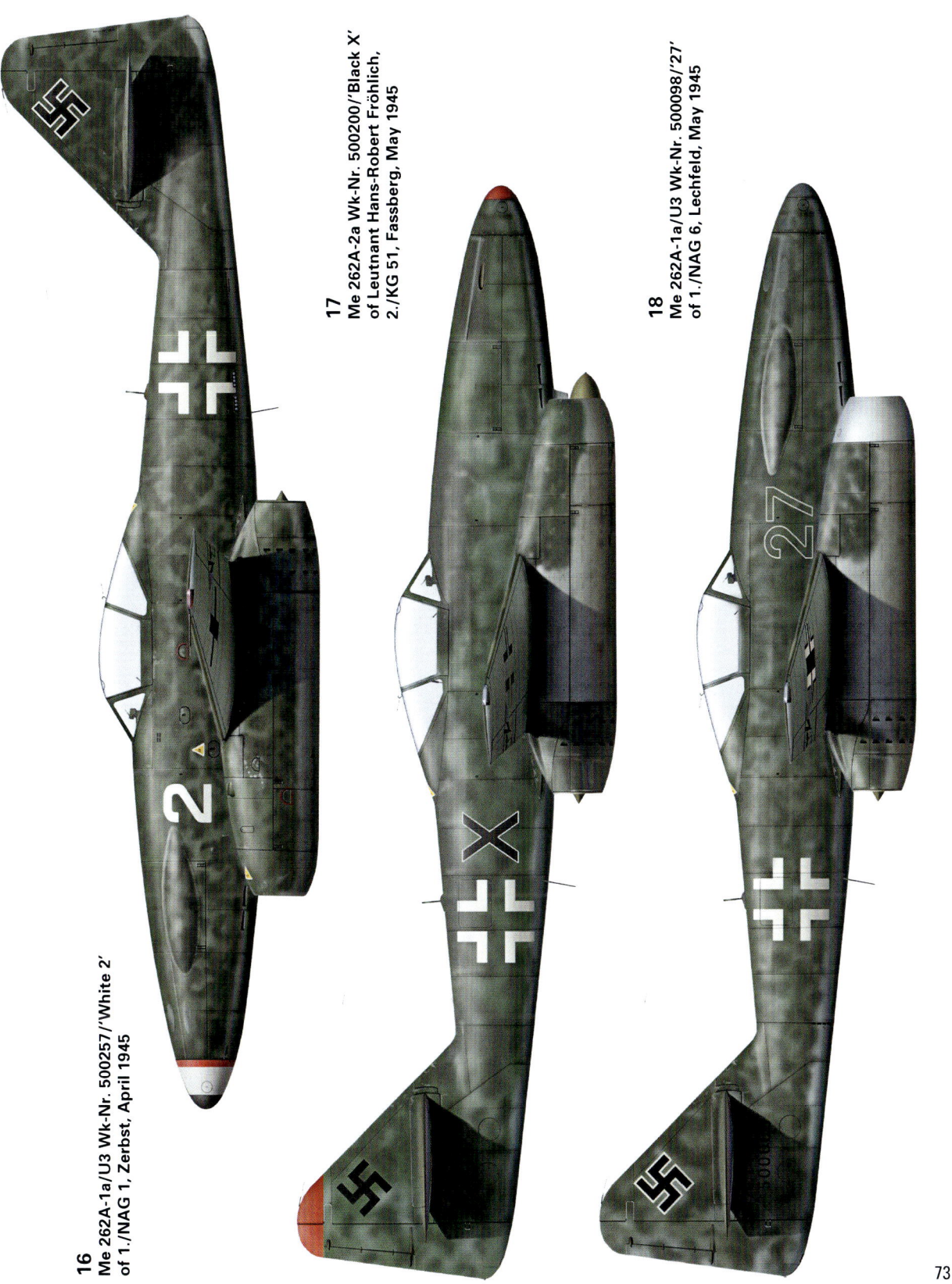

16
Me 262A-1a/U3 Wk-Nr. 500257/'White 2'
of 1./NAG 1, Zerbst, April 1945

17
Me 262A-2a Wk-Nr. 500200/'Black X'
of Leutnant Hans-Robert Fröhlich,
2./KG 51, Fassberg, May 1945

18
Me 262A-1a/U3 Wk-Nr. 500098/'27'
of 1./NAG 6, Lechfeld, May 1945

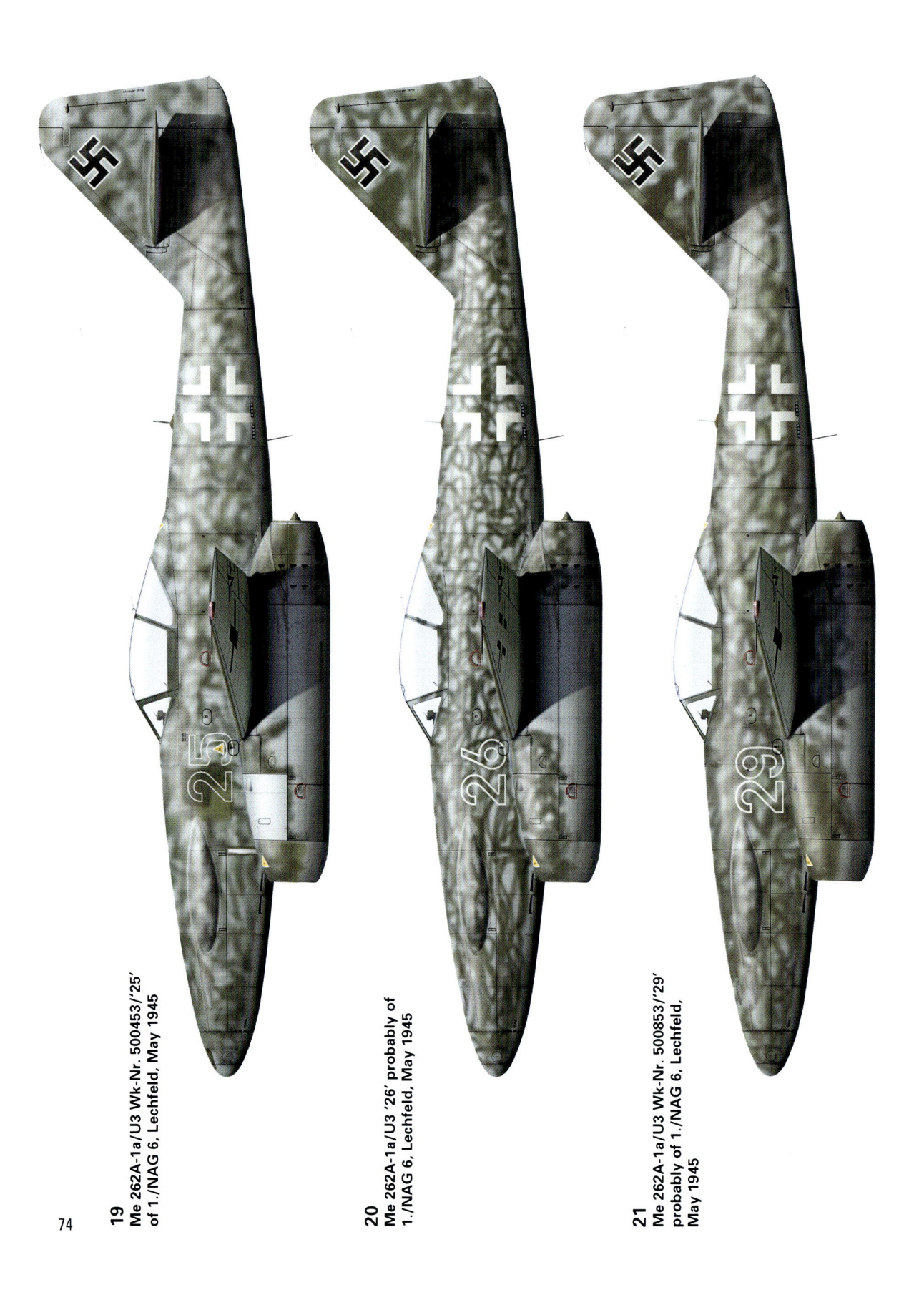

19
Me 262A-1a/U3 Wk-Nr. 500453/'25'
of 1./NAG 6, Lechfeld, May 1945

20
Me 262A-1a/U3 '26' probably of
1./NAG 6, Lechfeld, May 1945

21
Me 262A-1a/U3 Wk-Nr. 500853/'29'
probably of 1./NAG 6, Lechfeld,
May 1945

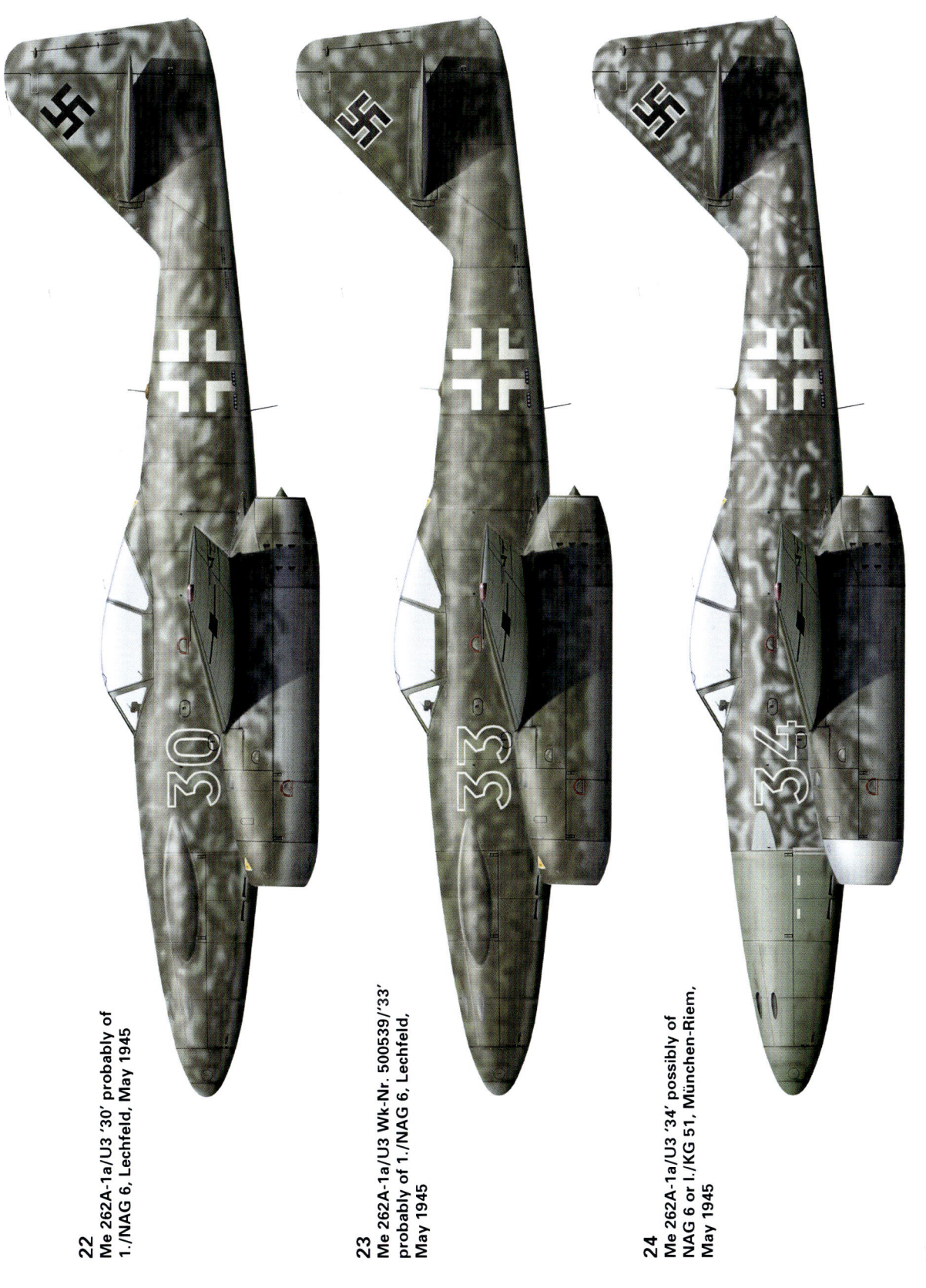

22
Me 262A-1a/U3 '30' probably of
1./NAG 6, Lechfeld, May 1945

23
Me 262A-1a/U3 Wk-Nr. 500539/'33'
probably of 1./NAG 6, Lechfeld,
May 1945

24
Me 262A-1a/U3 '34' possibly of
NAG 6 or I./KG 51, München-Riem,
May 1945

CHAPTER SIX

TOO LITTLE, TOO LATE

As the cold winter which heralded 1945 receded into a weak spring across northwest Europe, American forces took München-Gladbach on 1 March and at last reached the Rhine at Neuss, opposite Düsseldorf, on the 3rd. While on a tour of the Western Front, Winston Churchill visited the town of Jülich – he stood on German soil.

In the skies over the town, Allied air power was almost supreme. Almost. Together with the fighters of JGs 2, 26 and 53 by day, as well as the Ju 87s of NSGs 1 and 2 and the Fw 190s of NSGr 20 at night, the Me 262s of KG 51 commenced as concerted a campaign as possible against enemy breakthroughs in the area.

Between 0719-0742 hrs on the 1st, two Me 262s from KG 51, which was now operating under the command of *Luftflotte Reich*, flew a meteorological reconnaissance sortie in the Linnich area. Four SC 250 bombs were dropped on Linnich itself without any successes being observed. An hour later, three more jets from the unit flew operations against tank and troop concentrations in the Jüchen area. As the objective was not located, an alternative target at Düren was bombed.

Throughout the morning of the next day (2 March), 26 Me 262s from II./KG 51 at Mühlheim and 22 Ar 234s from III./KG 76 attacked tank and troop concentrations of the US Ninth Army in the Düren area. Attacks were made through flak against tank and troop assemblies at Rheindahlen (Leutnant Heid with SD 250 *Splitterbomben*), Erkelenz, Wickrath (Leutnant Lange), Bedburg and Elsdorf. Two Me 262s and one Ar 234 broke off the action due to technical faults, and II./KG 51 reported the Me 262A-2a of Hauptmann Fritz Abel, *Staffelkapitän* of 5./KG 51, lost. He had been shot down in the Aachen/Nijmegen area.

During the afternoon five Me 262s from II./KG 51 again targeted troops around Düren, with two jets over the town, one against Wickrath and one over Horrem (Feldwebel Groschopp). Ordnance was dropped from 4500 m down to 1500 m. No jets were lost to enemy action, but two Me 262A-2as had to break off owing to technical problems – they made emergency landings at Mühlheim. Unteroffizier Golde of 6. *Staffel* dropped his SD 250s in horizontal flight over Heppendorf. Other clashes took place between KG 51 and P-47s but without outcome. One USAAF fighter pilot reported that 'it was like rhinos chasing gazelles'.

Ground echelons of 2./NAG 6 arrived at Münster-Nord, but bad weather prevented the unit's Me 262s from making the journey. However, two sorties were made – one jet flew a visual reconnaissance of the Bischweiler-Zabern-Brumath area while another photographed roads in the Wantzenau, Zabern and Erstein areas. Likewise, on 3 March,

Hauptmann Dr Gutzmer of *Stab*/KG 51 flew an armed reconnaissance in the Grimlinghausen-Neuss-Büderich area, but this was considered only partially successful owing to bad weather.

Two days later units of the US VII Corps fought their way into Köln. Following an improvement in the weather, five Me 262s from I./KG 51, directed by 14. *Fliegerdivision*, took off to attack Allied troop concentrations on the road leading northwards out of Moers, but owing to heavy cloud, the target was not located. Three aircraft bombed secondary targets between Krefeld and Neuss, but no successes were observed. The remaining two aircraft broke off due to the bad weather, jettisoning their bombs. No losses were suffered.

For the next few days, the adverse weather grounded the jets. Meanwhile, as an indication of the desperate military predicament now facing the Third Reich, Göring called for volunteers from I./KG 51 at Hopsten to undertake self-sacrificial ramming operations against the great Ludendorff railway bridge at Remagen – a vital crossing point over the Rhine that the Americans had now reached and crossed. On 9 March, as Bonn and Bad Godesberg were captured by the US First Army, and other Allied forces continued to expand their bridgehead beyond the town, three Ar 234s from III./KG 76 attacked the bridge with 250 kg bombs, but without success. In response to Göring's call, two pilots from KG 51 came forward, but the suicide sortie was never flown.

Eight aircraft from *Gefechtsverband Kowalewski* made an attack on the Remagen Bridge on the 12th, seven aircraft bombing it and the other machine targeting transport columns. A second attack on the bridge was flown later by eight more aircraft from III./KG 76 and I./KG 51. No jets were lost, but no success was recorded either.

Taking off from Rheine on 13 March, four Me 262s from II./KG 51 made an attack between 0905 hrs and 1002 hrs at an altitude of 5000 m on river crossings in the bridgehead area. The jets were each equipped with two AB 250 containers filled with SD 10 anti-personnel bombs. A formation of ten P-47s was encountered, but it was to be a fruitless engagement for both sides. Due to the presence of the US fighters, the effects of bombing were not observed. Two jets were lost on the return flight to Rheine, one making an emergency landing near Lüdinghausen due to a shortage of fuel. The other pilot bailed out when an engine unit failed, his aircraft crashing at Neuenkirchen, southwest of Rheine.

Later in the day, 24 Me 262s from I. and II./KG 51 attacked enemy troop concentrations and road traffic in the Kleve-Xanten-Emmerich area. Two jets broke off due to technical defects and jettisoned their 500 kg containers of 10 kg anti-personnel bombs. Oberfähnrich Georg Schabinski of 5./KG 51 was injured on his return when his Me 262A-2a suffered a fuel problem and he had to crash near Coesfeld. Oberfähnrich Jürgen

A member of the groundcrew hand-signals airfield control from the port wing root of Me 262 'White C' of I./KG 51. The aircraft appears to be fitted with a single AB 500 bomb container, suggesting an imminent takeoff from its wet, mud-streaked airfield in early 1945

Höhne of 3./KG 51 was killed when his aircraft came down south of Xanten, his badly damaged jet later being discovered by advancing troops and inspected by Allied intelligence. Oberleutnant Harald Hovestadt, the *Gruppe* Adjutant of I./KG 51, was badly injured by flak as he and Leutnant Batel attacked vehicles northwest of Kalkar and southeast of Kleve. Both jets carried AB 250/SD 10 combinations. Hovestadt made it back to Hopsten, however, but was hospitalised.

Bad weather severely hampered combat flying over the next few days, but on the 18th operations resumed when, between 1138 hrs and 1238 hrs, three Me 262s of II./KG 51 mounted a high-level attack through clouds against the Remagen bridgehead from 6000 m using *Egon* control. Six 250 kg containers of SD 10 fragmentation bombs were dropped, but the effects were not observed. There was no contact with enemy aircraft. Simultaneously, two Me 262s of 6./KG 51 targeted vehicles northeast of Honnef, but one of the jets was unable to continue owing to *Egon* failure. The other dropped a 500 kg container of 10 kg fragmentation bombs from 6700 m, the effects not being observed.

The eventual capture of the Remagen Bridge rendered the airfields in the Rheine area untenable for the Luftwaffe and forced KG 51 to move, first to Giebelstadt and eventually to Leipheim, in Bavaria. The airfield at Giebelstadt was strafed by P-51s on 19 March and two Me 262s were destroyed, with another escaping with light damage. It is possible that some elements of KG 51 attempted to mount an operation against Allied advance columns in the Bad Kreuznach area that same day, but this was probably aborted. On the 20th an Me 262 did carry out an armed reconnaissance of the Kreuznach breakthrough point, however, the aircraft also dropping two 250 kg bombs on vehicle columns. The effects of this attack were not observed. This was followed by another pair of jets targeting troop concentrations in the same area, dropping two 250 kg bombs on enemy columns. There were no casualties.

On 14 March the *General der Aufklärer* ordered 1./NAG 1 at Herzogenaurach to relocate to Rhein-Main, while by the 10th most, if not all, of *Stab*, 1. and 2./NAG 6 had relocated to Münster-Handorf. The unit suffered the loss of Leutnant Walter Engelhart during this transfer on the 18th, when, flying at a height of just 150 m, his Me 262 rolled to the left and exploded when it hit the ground.

An Me 262 of NAG 6 was assigned to carry out a photo-reconnaissance mission over the Nijmegen-Emmerich-Goch-Kleve area on the 19th, but the sortie was aborted owing to heavy ground mist. However, another such sortie was sent out over the western bank of the Rhine from Xanten, south to Düsseldorf. An indication of just how important these reconnaissance operations were to the German high command can be seen by the fact that airfield cover for the missions was provided by no fewer than 27 Fw 190s of I. and IV./JG 26.

From left to right, Oberleutnant Harald Hovestadt (*Gruppe* Adjutant of I./KG 51), Hauptmann Rudolf Rösch (of 3./KG 51) and Major Heinz Unrau (the *Gruppenkommandeur*) are seen in buoyant mood in front of Me 262A-2a Wk-Nr. 170096 '9K+(white)BH' of 1./KG 51 at Rheine during the autumn of 1944. Hovestadt was wounded by ground fire during an attack on enemy vehicles near Kleve on 13 March 1945, and Rudolf Rösch was posted missing after his Me 262A-2a was hit by flak near Helmond on 28 November 1944 while on a weather reconnaissance flight. He had been awarded the Knight's Cross while serving as *Kapitän* of 9./KG 51 on 26 March 1944 following the completion of 100 combat missions and the rescuing of the crew of his then *Gruppenkommandeur* from its crash location 80 km behind enemy lines

On 20 March an Me 262 of NAG 6 flew a photo-reconnaissance sortie over the Reichswald-Xanten area, but the results it brought back were poor due to weather. The next day, with his jet training complete, Oberleutnant Erich Engels of 1./NAG 6 took off from Lechfeld in a factory-fresh Me 262 on course for Münster-Handorf, where he was to join his colleagues. The flight went without problems, and Engels landed and taxied his jet into a revetment. He shut down the engines and climbed out of the aircraft. As he made his way towards dispersal, the air raid alarm sounded and a few minutes later Allied bombs rained down on the airfield. Engels just had time to take cover. A short while later, after the bombers had departed, Engels was dismayed to discover that his new Me 262 had been a victim of the raid and was beyond saving.

A day or so later he journeyed to Rheine by car, where he collected a new Me 262 fighter which it was intended he would use for reconnaissance work. No sooner had Engels been assigned the jet than there was a request from the local army liaison unit for him to urgently conduct a reconnaissance flight to check on enemy forces in the Remagen area. From there he was to fly to Parchim. His flight completed, Engels headed for Parchim, but he found the field to be so badly damaged by bombs that he made for Hopsten. Even there conditions were bad, so he finally landed at Vörden, from where he eventually joined his comrades.

Overwhelming Allied air superiority and attrition was now making itself felt more than ever, and some saw KG 51's continued bomber operations as little more than futile. In late March, Generalleutnant Adolf Galland, the sacked *General der Jagdflieger* who had set up the new Me 262 fighter unit *Jagdverband* 44 at Brandenburg-Briest, visited Generalmajor Josef Kammhuber, Göring's 'Plenipotentiary for Jet Aircraft' at his HQ in Potsdam. Galland argued for the immediate cessation of bomber operations by KG 51 and the transfer to it of a number of experienced fighter pilots so that the unit's conversion to fighter operations could be put into effect. Galland seems to have failed in his request.

The war ground on. On 21 March, nearly 1300 heavy bombers from the Eighth Air Force targeted 11 jet airfields across northwest Germany, and with them came 750 P-51 escorts. Hesepe was 'visited' by 165 bombers, which used fragmentation bombs to destroy two jets and damage others parked in their dispersal areas, while Essen-Mühlheim was attacked by 90 bombers. At Hopsten, the runway was cratered and another two Me 262s destroyed. At Rheine, 180 bombers came in in two waves, dropping thousands of splinter and incendiary bombs. At Giebelstadt, Hauptmann Eberhard Winkel, *Staffelkapitän* of 3./KG 51, fell victim to a P-47 whilst taking off, and his *Staffel* comrade, Leutnant Erwin Diekmann, was also shot down and killed near the airfield. Winkel was replaced at the head of 3. *Staffel* by Oberleutnant Gustav Stephan.

Despite the bombing raids, a force of 27 Me 262s of KG 51 was despatched in four sorties throughout the day on ground-attack missions around Bad Kreuznach and Grünstadt. Two aircraft were forced to abort, but the remainder dropped 16 250 kg bombs and 26 250 kg containers loaded with 10 kg fragmentation bombs. They mounted attacks on road traffic, transport columns and concentrations of parked vehicles. Generally, effects were not observed, but several vehicles were seen to be on fire. There was no contact with the enemy.

CHAPTER SIX

On the 22nd, 18 Me 262s flew two ground-attack sorties at 0825 hrs and 0930 hrs. Three aircraft broke off, jettisoning their bombs in the process. The remaining jets dropped three 500 kg, seventeen 250 kg and two AB 250 containers with 10 kg bombs in glide attacks from altitudes of between 2500 m and 1800 m. Targets included occupied villages, road traffic, vehicle concentrations, two bridges and a flak battery. Once again, the success of the attacks could not be measured due to heavy flak, but in some cases large fires were seen. Unteroffizier Heinz Erben of 2. *Staffel* had only been airborne for three minutes after taking off for the mission when he was attacked by P-47s and crashed to his death near Wertheim.

The Me 262 reconnaissance force continued to be active. On 23 March *Stab*/NAG 1 was reported as transitioning onto the Me 262 at Lechfeld, and the *General der Aufklärer* issued orders that another reconnaissance *Staffel*, 1./NAG 13, should be assigned for conversion to the Me 262 also at Lechfeld. By the 25th, the *Staffel* was preparing to give up its Bf 109s at Oedheim for conversion to the jet.

Two days earlier, 2./NAG 6's Leutnante Schubert, Hader and Tetzner had been ordered to Lechfeld, where they collected new aircraft arriving from the plant at Eger, while Hauptmann Braunegg transferred with ground elements to Hildesheim. On the 24th an Me 262 of NAG 6 carried out reconnaissance over the Bocholt area between 0630 hrs and 0720 hrs, but the aircraft was destroyed when it force-landed – its pilot was unharmed. Another jet flew over the Wesel-Goch-Emmerich-Nijmegen area from 0730 hrs to 0820 hrs. On 26 March, between 1740 hrs and 1820 hrs, two Me 262s of NAG 6 carried out weather reconnaissance over Osnabrück and Soes, then headed south of Paderborn and west of Bielefeld. Only one jet was able to carry out partial coverage, however, owing to heavy cloud. That same day an Me 262 of 2./NAG 6 from Burg-bei-Magdeburg was lost when it suffered a heavy landing following an operation to the Bocholt area.

By the 27th, *Stab*/NAG 6 was at Vörden, 1./NAG 6 at Ahlhorn and 2./NAG 6 at Münster-Handorf, while on the 29th *Stab*/NAG 1

Personnel of 2./NAG 6 get to grips with a failed motor vehicle at Schwäbisch Hall in late 1944, very shortly before an Allied air attack on the airfield. They are, from second left to right, Leutnant Herbert Schubert (back to camera – pilot), Unterarzt Dr Wolfgang Riese (medical officer), Leutnant F W Schlüter (pilot) and Oberleutnant Erich Weiss (a unit staff officer). The small number of reconnaissance pilots of NAG 6 provided invaluable information to Wehrmacht commanders on the Western Front, but their effectiveness was restricted by modest resources, both in terms of aircraft and pilots

(with two jets) and 1. *Staffel* (with seven jets) were at Fritzlar-Nord.

During March, no fewer than 20 Me 262A-1a/U3 short-range reconnaissance jets were produced and delivered to NAGs' 6 and 1. Attempts to convert 1./NAG 13 seem to have faltered, however, 16. *Fliegerdivision* reporting that the *Staffel* remained without aircraft.

In the early morning of 26 March, in poor weather conditions, I./KG 51 began to relocate from Giebelstadt to Illesheim. The jet flown by Leutnant Heid developed a fire in one engine shortly after it had taken off, so he was forced to make an emergency landing at Waldmannshofen just five minutes after departing. Later that same morning, the weather slowly improved. Heinrich Haeffner recorded;

'The weather got somewhat better today, and so I took off armed with rockets and two bombs at 1121 hrs and headed to Seiligenstadt, where I bombed an American flak position. At 1154 hrs I landed back at Illesheim. However, the takeoff and landing were highly risky.'

The inference here is that Haeffner's jet had been armed with 55 mm R4M unguided rockets, which Me 262 fighter units JG 7 and JV 44 were deploying against heavy bombers. If this was the case, it was probably intended as a trial operation, using the rockets as ground-attack weapons.

During the afternoon Feldwebel Capitain and Leutnant Esche took off, aided by rocket-assistance, to attack a railway bridge near Aschaffenburg, each of their jets laden with one SC 250 and two SD 250 bombs. However, as Esche left the grass strip at Illesheim, the portside RATO unit fell away and his Me 262A-2a immediately lost power. Its landing gear struck the airfield boundary fence and the jet belly-landed. Fritz Esche quickly clambered out of his aircraft as it slid to a halt and he jumped into a small lake just as the Me 262 exploded. Capitain pressed on alone and carried out the mission, but on his return flight he encountered enemy fighters and his Me 262 received hits. He returned safely to Illesheim, however.

On 29 March two Me 262s from I./KG 51 undertook a weather and armed reconnaissance mission of the Hammelburg-Aschaffenburg-Worms area, although one aircraft had to break off. The remaining jet completed the sortie.

Hauptmann Herward Braunegg, *Staffelkapitän* of 2./NAG 6, prepares to put his 'foot to the pedal' in an attempt to get the problematic vehicle moving, while Leutnant F W Schlüter provides muscle power at the back, watched by Oberleutnant Erich Weiss and Unterarzt Dr Wolfgang Riese

Feldwebel Karl-Albrecht Capitain of 1. *Staffel* was one of the longest-serving and most active pilots in I./KG 51. Here he is opening the canopy of an Me 262

4., 5. and 6./KG 51 were all at Schwäbisch Hall on this date, with some remaining elements of II./KG 51 at Rheine. 4. and 6. *Staffeln* spent the day preparing to relocate to Unterschlauersbach, while 5./KG 51 was to move to München-Riem, where it would receive new Me 262s. At 1730 hrs on 30 March ground elements of II./KG 51 were ordered to transfer 'at once' to Unterschlauersbach in vehicles provided by *Gefechtsverband Kowalewski*.

On the last day of the month KG 51 reported having 79 Me 262s on strength. The *Geschwader* was now placed under the tactical control of IX. *Fliegerkorps (J.)*, and it was to undertake operations in the defence of the Reich as briefed by Generalmajor Kammhuber. However, in the early morning, and as its last order to KG 51, 16. *Fliegerdivision* directed the *Geschwader* to send all available aircraft to attack the bridges around Hanau and Allied troops in the Mannheim-Heidelburg area. Twelve aircraft from I./KG 51 duly took off from Leipheim and targeted bridges and enemy troops between 0607 hrs and 0850 hrs. Three aircraft dropped two 250 kg bombs each and another an AB 250 container holding SD 10 anti-personnel bombs. A fifth jet expended an AB 500 container with the same SD 10 load on the pontoon bridge south of Hanau. Thick fog obscured the results of the attack.

The Me 262A-2a of Leutnant Lange of 1./KG 51 was hit by flak during his glide-attack through fog at 1000 m over the target, but he released his SD 250s and returned safely. Three more aircraft dropped a total of two AB 250 containers and one AB 500 container on another temporary bridge west of Hanau, hits on enemy troops on the bridge being observed. Two more jets from I./KG 51 dropped 250 kg bombs on a transport column south of Hanau, but another machine was forced to break off its attack due to a technical fault. No losses were suffered.

Three Me 262s from I. *Gruppe* flew a further similar mission between 1107 hrs and 1158 hrs. One of these aircraft dropped a 250 kg bomb on the bridge west of Hanau, and another made an attack on a stationary transport column west of the town. The third machine was forced to break off due to a technical failure. Again, no losses were sustained. II./KG 51 was also involved in similar operations.

In the afternoon, a third mission was mounted by Leutnant Lange and Feldwebel Capitain with SD 250s against columns on the road from Amorbach to Walldürn. Over the target, Capitain's Me 262A-1a was fired upon by enemy fighters and flak, while Lange attacked a convoy of 16 vehicles southeast of Rippberg-im-Odenwald with his Me 262A-2a in a gliding attack from 2000 m, releasing his ordnance at 1300 m. While in the target area, he was attacked by six P-47s, but was able to out-manoeuvre them. Both Capitain and Lange returned safely to Leipheim.

Heinrich Haeffner recalled;

'We transferred our machines from Illesheim to Leipheim, on the Donau. Other machines from the *Gruppe* had already transferred there. The airfield had already been badly hit by the Americans, but the centre lane of the nearby Autobahn was concrete so we were able to take off and land on it. The fuel and service station was made into a command post for the *Gruppe*. If at all possible, the pilots tried to land back on the grass airfield, since their landing wheels would run too fast on the concrete of the Autobahn.'

Under the watchful gaze of its groundcrew, Me 262A-1a/U3 'White 2' of 1./NAG 1 prepares to move off at the start of another photo-reconnaissance sortie from Zerbst in early April 1945. Clearly visible is the bulged fairing on the nose to allow fitment of an Rb 50/30 camera. The nose tip is adorned in three separate colours

Oberfeldwebel Fritz Oldenstädt of 2./NAG 6 flew some of the last Luftwaffe jet reconnaissance sorties of the war

In the afternoon, jets from II./KG 51 targeted American troops near Hardheim, northeast of Walldürn, after which they returned to Unterschlauersbach.

In the first few days of April 1945 – the penultimate month of the war – Adolf Hitler had moved his headquarters to a bunker deep beneath his Chancellery in Berlin. On the Western Front, Allied forces had completed their encirclement of the Ruhr. The end of the Thousand-Year Reich was in sight, but the crews of the Luftwaffe's jet bomber and reconnaissance units flew and fought on in their final battles.

On the 1st, 19 Me 262s of KG 51 made gliding attacks with SD 250s and AB 250/SD 10s against enemy columns and positions west of Würzburg-Bad Mergentheim. After dropping their bombs, some jets strafed the targets at low level. The *Geschwader* made attacks on other targets during the day too.

Oberleutnant Ernst Bratke of NAG 6 took off from Vörden for a reconnaissance operation in the Münster area. On his return flight he hit bad weather, lost his orientation and began to run out of fuel near Brockum. He was killed attempting an emergency landing in the Dummer See/Oldenburg area. At this time the *Stab* and 1./NAG 6 (with no aircraft) were based at Lechfeld, while 2./NAG 6, with eight aircraft, was at Kaltenkirchen and Hohne. 1./NAG 1 was ordered to Zerbst with its Me 262s on the 1st and arrived there the next day.

With the need to strengthen the Me 262 fighter units, on 2 April I./KG 51 was ordered to transfer some of its aircraft to JG 7 at Burg-bei-Magdeburg, Oranienburg and Rechlin. II./KG 51 was apparently at Hörsching under the command of IX. *Fliegerkorps (J.)*.

Oberfeldwebel Fritz Oldenstädt of 2./NAG 6 took off during the evening of the 2nd on a reconnaissance of the Paderborn-Kassel area, but shortly after leaving the ground a large flame was seen trailing from his Me 262's left engine. Oldenstädt took emergency procedures and forced-landed at Heeke, wrecking the aircraft. The next day, *Stab*/NAG 6 moved to Fassberg. On the 5th it seems *Stab* and 1./NAG 6 finally obtained some jets, for 'four available' Me 262s conducted reconnaissance flights over the Ruhr, Lüneberg Heath and Magdeburg.

By the 6th 1./NAG 1, under 15. *Fliegerdivision*, was operational with seven Me 262s at Zerbst, although only three of the jets were serviceable. The unit was to cover the 'central area as far west as Frankfurt/Main'. A *Rotte*, consisting of one fighter and one reconnaissance aircraft, flew 1./NAG 1's first sortie. The unit also 'borrowed' an Me 262B-1a trainer from III./EJG 2 – one of seven such aircraft that the latter *Gruppe* had 'handed over to operational units', leaving it with 'none left'. Prevailing operating conditions were illustrated by reports from Lechfeld on 8 April that eight pilots of 1./NAG 1 were training on the borrowed Me 262. The *Staffel* flew a reconnaissance operation of the Mülhausen-Langensalza-Gotha area between 0805 hrs and 0856 hrs, but sorties by three other aircraft between 0800 hrs and 0900 hrs were broken off due to technical failures.

Also on the 8th, *Stab*/NAG 1 was ordered to join 1. *Staffel* at Zerbst, 2./NAG 1 was to go to Körnelitz and 3./NAG 1 to Altengrabow. Meanwhile, on the 9th, *Stab*/NAG 6 was at Lechfeld under Major Heinz Schultze – but without aircraft – along with 2./NAG 6 under Herward Braunegg, which had seven Me 262s (three serviceable). I./KG 51 was at Leipheim under Major Unrau with 15 Me 262s (11 serviceable) and II./KG 51 was at Linz and Hörsching under Hauptmann Grundmann with six jets (two serviceable). Up to 10 April, KG 51 had apparently received a total allocation of 242 Me 262s. Of this number, 88 had been lost through enemy activity and 146 to other reasons!

On 10 April I. *Gruppe* flew sorties against Allied troops advancing in the Crailsheim area in the early morning. Heinrich Haeffner recalled;

'I received a new Me 262. Our aircraft were hidden in the forest to the left and right of the Autobahn. American fighters were constantly over our airfield and Marauder units carpeted the field with bombs. At 1106 hrs, I took off from the Autobahn for a mission to Crailsheim. The aircraft was pulled onto the Autobahn with a *Kettenkrad*. Then the turbines were started and we headed off on an easterly course. The landing took place from the west so that we could quickly be hidden again in the forest. I was elated not to have become easy prey for enemy fighters on landing. At 1419 hrs, I took off again with two 250 kg bombs towards Roth, near Nürnberg. I attacked a bridge there. At 1716 hrs I flew another mission to Roth. There was a lot of flak in the target area.'

More than 1315 bombers, supported by 905 fighters from the Eighth Air Force, targeted jet airfields in northern Germany on the 10th. At Burg, the USAAF unloaded hundreds of tons of bombs in a 20-minute assault that prevented the base from being used again until war's end. Ten Me 262s were destroyed on the ground, including three from 2./NAG 6. The *Staffel* subsequently moved, by way of Fassberg, to join the remainder of the *Gruppe* at Lechfeld. Jets from the unit then carried out reconnaissance of the Minden-Hildesheim-Celle and Verden areas.

Generalmajor Kammhuber, as Göring's jet aircraft 'Plenipotentiary', emphasised to his units on the 11th the need for 'utmost economy in use of J2 [fuel]. Waste must not continue. Aircraft are not to taxi to parking places under their own power. Unit commanders are to be instructed under threat of court martial'.

'I was able to make another operational flight in the Nürnberg area', Heinrich Haeffner of 2./KG 51 recorded on 11 April. 'I landed well on the Autobahn at 0958 hrs and vanished with my machine into the forest. Enemy fighters are always in the sky'. His *Gruppe* reported 16 Me 262s on strength, of which ten were serviceable, but there was some confusion as to which command actually controlled the *Geschwader* tactically at this point – *Luftwaffenkommando West* or IX. *Fliegerkorps* (J).

Meanwhile, the disbanding KG(J) 55, which had begun to train up on the Me 262, was ordered to hand over its vehicles and equipment to II./KG 51. This seems to have been a pointless order, for II. *Gruppe* had just been instructed to surrender all of its aircraft to other units!

NAG 1 was told by 15. *Fliegerdivision* to undertake reconnaissance of the Harz area in order to photograph Allied armoured spearheads, and to cover up to 30 km in the enemy rear. Coverage was also to be flown in the Göttingen-Northeim and Langensalza-Erfurt areas, as well as over the roads around Marburg-Giessen and Friedburg. Reconnaissance missions were to continue regularly from then on, weather permitting.

One Me 262 from KG 51 made a weather reconnaissance over the Western Front – or what remained of it – on 14 April, while six jets from I. *Gruppe* attacked troop movements in the Rastatt/Baden-Baden area, and hits were seen on vehicles. By the 17th the Me 262 units had settled in at their new bases, with *Stab* and I./KG 51 at Leipheim, II./KG 51 at Landau, *Stab*/NAG 6 at Kaltenkirchen, 1./NAG 6 at Hahn and 2./NAG 6 at Rechlin-Lärz. NAG 1 lost two Me 262s during its transfer to its new base at Eger, one of which was flown by Oberfeldwebel Peter Wilke of the *Stab*. His rare Me 262A-4 was shot down over Cheb. These jets may have fallen victim to P-47s of the 362nd or 371st FGs.

Seven Me 262s from I./KG 51 attacked columns of the US Seventh Army in the Nuremberg area in three separate operations during the morning of the 18th. An air battle ensued with eight P-51s as the jets approached the target area, one Mustang being downed (probably from the 339th FG). At least one of these missions was led by Wilhelm Batel. During the afternoon, Karl-Albrecht Capitain of 1./KG 51 attacked columns on the Reichsautobahn at Lauf-an-der-Pegnitz, northeast of Nuremberg. Fired at by flak in the target area, Capitain was also attacked by fighters, but without success. He dropped two SD 250s on vehicles and returned safely to Leipheim. Similarly, Oberfeldwebel Hieronymus Lauer of 3./KG 51 struck at the same target later that evening and also encountered Mustangs. He managed to shoot one P-51 down.

Two days later the *Geschwader* suffered a severe blow when its *Kommodore*, Oberstleutnant Rudolf Hallensleben, holder of the Knight's Cross, was killed when his vehicle was strafed by USAAF fighters on the Autobahn bridge over the Donau near Leipheim. Three of his staff were also killed. Command of KG 51 was assumed by the *Kommandeur* of IV. *Gruppe*, Major Siegfried 'Balbo' Barth – another Knight's Cross-holder and a veteran of the *Edelweiss Geschwader* since May 1939.

On 20 April the pilots of KG 51 were literally combating the enemy on their doorstep, with attacks being made on enemy vehicles nearing Leipheim. That day a transfer began to Memmingen. It was ordered that, if possible, a small rear detachment was to be left at the airfield to repair unserviceable aircraft and blow up the rest. II.*Gruppe* was to move to Strasskirchen or Linz/Hörsching, while IV./KG 51 remained at Neuburg-an-der-Donau in only *Staffel* strength. 7. *Jagddivision*, in tactical control of KG 51, ordered the *Geschwaderstab* to transfer to Rosenheim. Upon transferring to Memmingen on the 21st, however, Oberleutnant Haeffner lamented 'the bomb craters there were so badly repaired that I damaged my nose wheel on landing'. That day the *Geschwader* had attacked enemy columns at Göppingen in cooperation with Bf 109s of JG 53.

I./KG 51 flew fighter-bomber sorties against the bridgeheads at Dillingen on the Donau, northwest of Augsburg, on the 22nd, as well as cannon attacks against American troop concentrations west of Memmingen. However, a large element of II./KG 51, including the *Kommandeur*, Hauptmann Grundmann, was apparently captured at Strasskirchen by tanks of the US Seventh Army. Next day, the *Gruppe* reported just two Me 262s on strength with 34 pilots at Landau/Isar.

As the French First Army advanced southeastwards, I./KG 51 managed to get clear of Memmingen at the last moment with its aircraft and ground staff under the command of Major Brücker. The *Gruppe* flew two sorties against the Danube bridges at Dillingen before transferring to München-Riem, where it handed over its nine airworthy Me 262s to JV 44 and was effectively disbanded. Paradoxically though, the previous day JV 44 had requested that 'it be sent no more aircraft since it did not have the facilities to handle them'. Two jets came to München-Riem from II./KG 51 at Landau but were not taken over by Galland's *Verband*.

Constant fighter-bomber attacks at the new base made it impossible for the unit's pilots to carry out any meaningful operations. Adolf Galland, CO of JV 44, once remarked that at Riem, US fighter-bombers 'would even attack a stray dog'. In any case, it is unlikely that there was any ordnance for the *Gruppe* to utilise there. On the 24th, KG 51, as an independent fighting force, was declared 'disbanded'. All personnel equipped with arms were 'to be subordinated to ground organisation, while personnel without arms to be placed on the Army Reserve'. Thus began the end of the six-year history of the '*Edelweiss*' *Geschwader*.

In a twist on 26 April, however, OKL rescinded the disbandment and ordered I./KG 51 to be sent to Prague-Ruzyne, without its technical personnel, from where it would support operations in the battle for Berlin. Subsequently, in the confusing mesh of orders circulating amidst the disintegrating command structure, *Luftflottenkommando* 6 had ordered the 7. *Jagddivision* to return all Me 262s previously handed over to JV 44 to I./KG 51 at Holzkirchen, which was then to transfer to Prague-Ruzyne, where it would be placed under the command of IX. *Fliegerkorps* (J). During the transfer flight the jets were to attack enemy troops in the Regen area. However, the transfer was postponed due to inclement weather, and it is unlikely that the unit regained its Me 262s.

It was intended that the remnants of I./KG 51, together with I. and II./KG(J) 54 and III./KG(J) 6, were to combine at Prague-Ruzyne as *Gefechtsverband Hogeback*. Led by the illustrious *Kommodore* of KG(J) 6, Oberstleutnant Hermann Hogeback, this combat group was also joined by jet fighters from JG 7. Thirty-one aircraft from the ad hoc grouping flew ground attack missions in the Cottbus-Bautzen area, destroying two

In late April 1945, elements of I./KG 51 moved to München-Riem, where they were under orders to make their aircraft available to Generalleutnant Adolf Galland's *Jagdverband* 44 as fighters. This is Me 262A-1a Wk-Nr. 110836 'Black L' of 2./KG 51 seen after it had landed at Riem. The aircraft would be flown by Hauptmann Rudolf Abrahamczik, commander of 2./KG 51, on 8 May – the last day of the war – when he transferred it from Saaz to Riem, having spent a brief period operating from Prague-Ruzyne

aircraft and six motor vehicles with R4M rockets, but it is unlikely that jets from KG 51 were involved by this stage.

Ironically, it was no less a figure than SS-*Obergruppenführer* Hans Kammler, Hitler's personal 'Plenipotentiary for Jet Aircraft', who signalled Göring, warning him that it was impossible for the jet units to remain in Prague-Ruzyne due to there being only enough fuel for 'one operation'. Since timely supply by rail could not be guaranteed and delivery by road tanker was no longer possible, the fuel that remained would be needed for a further transfer in any case. Nor was there adequate flak protection in Prague, and supplies of spare parts, repair workshops and industry had mostly been transferred south. Furthermore, Kammler considered any suggestion of a transfer of these units to the north impossible since it was the shared opinion of the jet unit commanders now based on fields around the Czech capital that continued Me 262 operations depended largely on the expertise of qualified technical personnel who did not exist in the north.

At this time, the Me 262 units still operational in any way were *Stab* and 2./NAG 6 at Schleswig and 1./NAG 6 at Höhn, near Rendsburg, while 1./NAG 1 was at Rechlin. On 24 April Hauptmann Dünkel of the latter unit flew a reconnaissance patrol along the stretch of the Elbe between Wittenberg and Magdeburg. The *Stab* and II./KG 51 were committed to 'ground fighting' and, as noted, parts of I. *Gruppe* were either at Riem or Prague-Ruzyne.

Despite Kammler's caution, on 28 April *Luftflottenkommando* 6 instructed Galland by telephone to arrange the transfer of all JG 7 and KG 51 crews still at Riem to Prague-Ruzyne as soon as the prevailing poor weather permitted. Due to the weather, an interim landing field at Hörsching was proposed where there was 439 cbm of J2 jet fuel. The next day, some KG 51 pilots took their aircraft back from JV 44 at Riem in readiness for the transfer to Prague-Ruzyne.

On 30 April nine jets led by Hauptmann Abrahamczik, commander of 2./KG 51, transferred from Hörsching to Prague-Ruzyne airfield. The eight other pilots were Hauptmann Otto Christoph, Oberleutnant Heinz Strothmann (2. *Staffel*), Leutnant Batel (*Stab* I./KG 51), Oberleutnant Haeffner (2. *Staffel*), Leutnant Anton Schimmel (1. *Staffel*), Oberfeldwebel Hans-Robert Fröhlich (10. *Staffel*), Oberfeldwebel Helmut Bruhn (1. *Staffel*) and Unteroffizier Eberhard Pöhling (6. *Staffel*). Upon their arrival at Prague-Ruzyne at 2100 hrs, they were placed under the command of Hogeback and some, if not all, of their aircraft were fitted with wooden underwing launch racks for 55 mm R4M rockets. The KG 51 pilots could not believe their eyes at the 'peacetime conditions' existing on the airfield, with German aircraft neatly lined up in the open.

Gefechtsverband Hogeback flew determined, if hopeless, ground-

Members of Maj Harold E Watson's 54th Air Disarmament Squadron – dubbed 'Watson's Whizzers' – gather for a snapshot along with two German test pilots, Willie Hofmann and Karl Baur, in June 1945. The men are standing in front of a column of captured Me 262s ready to be flown from Lechfeld to Melun, in France, in preparation for eventual shipment to America. The aircraft closest to the camera is Me 262A-1a/U3 'Red 27', which was possibly from NAG 6. It had been given the name *Joanne* by the Americans following its capture. After arrival in the USA, having been renamed *Cookie VII*, the aircraft was written off when it crashed in Pittsburgh while being flown on a ferry flight by Lt James Holt

attack operations using R4M rockets against Soviet troops in the battle for Berlin, but following the fall of the capital, operations were restricted to the area around Prague. During the evening of 5 May, Prague-Ruzyne airfield came under artillery fire. The next day, orders were issued to evacuate. A small operational detachment from KG 51 under Hauptmann Abrahamczik moved to Saaz, where it flew close support operations around the Prague area.

Heinrich Haeffner recalled;

'During the afternoon [of 6 May] the weather improved just as General Peltz landed at Prague-Ruzyne. He ordered all jets to transfer to Saaz. KG 51 was to fly a mission to Brünn and then land at Saaz. I took off at 1619 hrs with 24 55 mm rockets, two cannon loaded with 100 rounds of 3 cm shells and 500 kg of bombs in a canister of 10 kg bombs.

'Shortly after takeoff, I heard on the radio that we were to call off the attack on Brünn and instead were to attack elements of the Vlasov Army on the road from Pilsen to Prague. After the attack, all aircraft were to return to Prague-Ruzyne. Gen Vlasov's troops were mutinous and were attacking German troops [rather than the Red Army, as they had been trained to do]. I changed course and looked for the road from Pilsen to Prague. Soon I saw the vehicle and tank columns of the Vlasov Army. In a low-level attack, I dropped canisters of anti-personnel bombs. During my second attack, I used my rockets against trucks and tanks. During my third attack, I emptied my cannon. Many trucks were in flames. At least 30 Me 262s participated in this attack.

'Around 1900 hrs, I was ordered to destroy "Radio Prague" with my Me 262. This radio station had constantly called for an uprising by the Czech population against the Germans, and it also called upon the RAF for help. On a map of the city, I was shown the exact location of the radio station. At 1950 hrs, I started with two 250 kg high explosive bombs and 24 rockets. I clearly recognised the target and dropped my bombs in two attacks. During a third attack, I launched all my rockets. At 2035 hrs I landed at Prague-Ruzyne unharmed. There were no transmissions from "Radio Prague" that night.'

In local operations, Leutnant Schimmel was lost in his Me 262A-1a to ground fire on 6 May, his jet crashing into the city streets below, while on the 7th, Oberleutnant Strothmann and Unteroffizier Pöhling, both flying Me 262A-1as, were posted missing.

The battle for Prague-Ruzyne waged until 7 May, when the men of the *Gefechtsverband* braced themselves for the inevitable overrunning of the field by the enemy. Following orders to destroy all non-serviceable aircraft, the remaining jets of *Gefechtsverband Hogeback* took off for Saaz. There, on 8 May, Hauptmann Abrahamczik gave the final orders to the pilots of KG 51 when he told them to fly their Me 262s to fields occupied by the Western Allies. Leutnant Fröhlich went to Fassberg, along with aircraft from JG 7, Leutnant Batel set course for Lüneburg, while Abrahamczik and Oberleutnant Haeffner (using jets from III./KG(J) 6) flew to München-Riem.

The Me 262 reconnaissance units also kept operating up to the end. On 1 May, Leutnant Tetzner of 2./NAG 6 made his last flight from Kaltenkirchen over Hannover-Magdeburg-Schwerin-Lübeck before landing at Schleswig-Land (Jagel). Over Bad Oldesloe he had spotted

Oberfeldwebel Hans-Robert Fröhlich flew Me 262A-2a '9K+(Black)XK' as part of the 2./KG 51 contingent of *Gefechtsverband Hogeback* in May 1945

A British soldier ropes off Me 262A-2a, W.Nr.500200, '9K+(Black)XK', of 2./KG 51 at Fassberg on 8 May 1945. The aircraft had just been flown in by Fahnenjunker-Oberfeldwebel Hans-Robert Fröhlich from Prague-Ruzyne as part of a group of Me 262s of Gefechstverband Hogeback. The aircraft was marked initially by the British as 'Air.Min 81' and subsequently flown by the RAE from September 1945 before being shipped to Australia in late 1946. At the time of writing it is on display at the Australian War Memorial in Canberra.

The wingless remains of the fuselage of Me 262 'Black O', which was assigned to Leutnant Heinrich Haeffner of 2./KG 51, were photographed abandoned in a scrap area at Saaz, in Bohemia-Moravia, in 1945. The other fuselages represent aircraft from KG(J) 6 and JG 7

two British fighters 200 metres away to the side of him, but he chose not to engage them and flew off into the cover of cloud.

On the 4th, on orders from his *Kommandeur*, Major Schultze, Oberfeldwebel Oldenstädt flew the last reconnaissance mission from Höhn that evening. On the morning of the 5th, Schultze and Oldenstädt received orders to fly in a two-seat Me 262 to Norway, but the aircraft's engines were faulty and so they were unable to execute the order. In the late morning British tanks reached the airfield, and the German airmen set about blowing up their aircraft.

At dawn on 7 May 1945, Oberleutnant Haeffner of 2./KG 51 prepared himself for what was to be his last ground-attack mission;

'At first light the groundcrew got my machine ready for takeoff. As I climbed into my aircraft and the Riedel motor was started, there was the first sound of machine gun fire. However, I brought both turbines up to full power and I took off immediately. I attacked enemy troops south of the airfield with bombs, rockets and cannon.'

Haeffner was in the air for 45 minutes, landing at 0610 hrs. He took off on a second sortie over the airfield at 1025 hrs, but received light damage from ground fire to his aircraft as he got airborne. He flew over the enemy positions and fired rockets into their vehicles, before heading for Saaz. By the time Haeffner had landed, his Me 262 had suffered so much battle damage that it was not repairable.

In the last mention of the jet bomber and reconnaissance units, on 8 May 1945 7. *Jagddivision* at Saalbach told *Luftwaffenkommando West* at Lofer that I., II. and 13./KG 51 were without aircraft at Holzkirchen and listed as being on *'Streifendienst'* – patrol duty around the airfield. *Luftflottenkommando Reich* reported that both the *Stab* and 2./NAG 6 were at Schleswig and 1./NAG 6 at Höhn 'grounded'. Despite fighting to the bitter end, their efforts had been too little, too late.

APPENDICES

UNIT STRUCTURE AND BASES – Me 262 OPERATIONAL PERIOD MID-1944 TO MAY 1945

Einsatzkommando Schenck

Kommandoführer	6-9/44	Major Wolfgang Schenck

Known bases:

20/6/44 to 20/7/1944	Lechfeld
20/7/44 to 12/8/44	Châteaudun
12/8/44 to 15/8/44	Etampes
15/8/44 to 22/8/44	Creil
22/8/44 to 28/8/44	Juvincourt
28/8/44 to 30/8/44	Ath-Chièvres
30/8/44 to 5/9/44	Volkel and Eindhoven
5/9/44 to ?	Rheine

Kampfgeschwader 51

Stab/KG 51

Kommodore	to 20/10/44	Major Wolf-Dietrich Meister
	21/10/44 to 31/1/45	Major Wolfgang Schenck
	1/2/45 to 9/4/45	Oberstleutnant Rudolf Hallensleben
	19/4/45 to 28/4/45	Oberstleutnant Siegfried Barth
Adjutant	to 25/1/45	Hauptmann Bernhard Sartor
	26/1/45 to 28/4/45	Hauptmann Dr Hans Gutzmer
Ia (Operations)	to 4/10/44	Hauptmann Hans-Joachim Grundmann
IT (Technical)	to 31/12/44	Hauptmann Hans-Joachim Bauer
	1/1/45 to 8/5/45	Leutnant Wilhelm Batel

Known bases:

23/5/44 to ?/8/44	Lechfeld
8/44 to 11/44	Landsberg/Lech
11/44 to 20/3/45	Rheine and Hopsten
20/3/45 to 30/3/45	Giebelstadt
30/3/45 to 21/4/45	Leipheim
21/4/45 to 24/4/45	Memmingen
24/4/45 to 30/4/45	Holzkirchen

Stab I./KG 51

Kommandeur	to 28/4/45	Major Heinz Unrau
Adjutant	15/10/44 to 28/4/45	Oberleutnant Harald Hovestadt
Ia	to 13/11/44	Oberleutnant Rudolf Merlau
	14/11/44 to 28/4/45	Oberleutnant Albersmeier
Ic (Intelligence)	?/44 to 21/3/45	Oberleutnant Gustav Stephan
IT	?/44 to 31/12/44	Leutnant Wilhelm Batel
	1/1/45 to 28/4/45	Hauptmann Hans-Joachim Bauer

1./KG 51

Staffelkapitän	19/4/44 to 28/4/45	Hauptmann Georg Csurusky

2./KG 51

Staffelkapitän	to 8/10/44	Hauptmann Gerhard Müller
	9/10/44 to 8/5/45	Hauptmann Rudolf Abrahamczik

3./KG 51

Staffelkapitän	to 4/9/44	Hauptmann Hans Gutzmer
	5/9/44 to 21/3/45	Hauptmann Eberhard Winkel
	22/3/45 to 28/4/45	Oberleutnant Gustav Stephan

Known bases:

23/5/44 to 20/7/44	Lechfeld/Leipheim
20/7/44 to 12/8/44	Châteaudun
12/8/44 to 15/8/44	Etampes
15/8/44 to 27/8/44	Creil
27/8/44 to 28/8/44	Juvincourt
28/8/44 to 30/8/44	Ath-Chièvres
30/8/44 to 5/9/44	Volkel
5/9/44 to 20/3/45	Rheine and Hopsten
20/3/45 to 30/3/45	Giebelstadt
30/3/45 to 21/4/45	Leipheim
21/4/45 to 24/4/45	Memmingen
24/4/45 to 30/4/45	München-Riem
30/4/45 to 6/5/45	Prague-Ruzyne (remains of 2./KG 51)
6/5/45 to 8/5/45	Saaz (remains of 2./KG 51)

Stab II./KG 51

Kommandeur	11/10/44 to 24/4/45	Hauptmann Hans-Joachim Grundmann
Adjutant	to 24/4/45	Hauptmann Willi Berberich/ Oblt Bubenick
Ia	?	Leutnant Egon Schlegel?
Ic	to 31/12/44	Oberleutnant Martin Kneiss
IT	15/12/44 to 24/4/45	Oberleutnant Hermann Walther

Known bases:

15/8/44 to 31/12/44	Schwäbisch Hall (6./KG 51 at Hesepe 21/12/44 to 10/1/45)
31/12/44 to 10/1/45	Achmer
10/1/45 to 21/3/45	Essen-Mühlheim
21/3/45 to 30/3/45	Schwäbisch Hall
30/3/45 to ?/4/45	Fürth
?/4/45 to 24/4/45	Linz/Hörsching

4./KG 51

Staffelkapitän	8/12/44 to 25/12/44	Oberleutnant Hans-Georg Lamle
	26/12/44 to 24/4/45	Leutnant Ewald Gersch

5./KG 51

Staffelkapitän	15/10/44 to 2/3/45	Hauptmann Friedrich Abel
	4/3/45 to 24/4/45	Hauptmann Friedrich Senne

6./KG 51

Staffelkapitän	15/10/44 to 24/4/45	Oberleutnant Wolfgang Baetz

Sonderkommando Braunegg
(***Kommando Panther*** **from November 1944**)

Kommandoführer	?/11/44 to 6/2/45	Oberleutnant Herward Braunegg
Known bases:	6/44 to 11(?)/44	Lechfeld
	11/44	Schwäbisch Hall and Münster-Handorf(?)

***Nahaufklärungsgruppe* 1**

Kommandeur	from 10/44 to 5/45	Major Werner Wilke

1./NAG 1

Staffelkapitän		Oberleutant Wilhelm Knoll
Known bases:	8/44 to 25/2/45	Bayreuth-Bindlach
	25/2/45 to 3/45	Hennef
	4/45	Zerbst
	3/45 to 5/45	Fritzlar

***Nahaufklärungsgruppe* 6**

Kommandeur	circa 20/1/45 to 5?/45	Major Friedrich Heinz Schultze

1./NAG 6

Staffelkapitän	?/45	Oberleutnant Georg Keck
Gefechtsstand (HQ)		Leutnant Heinz Plieth
TO (Technical)		Oberleutnant Emil Langendorf
Known bases:	8/44 to 2/9/44	Bayreuth-Bindlach
	2/9/44 to 12/44	Herzogenaurach
	12/44 to 28/2/45	Lechfeld
	28/2/45 to 27/3/45	Schwäbisch Hall
	27/3/45 to 12/4/45	Lechfeld
	12/4/45 to 2/5/45	Kaltenkirchen
	2/5/45 to 8/5/45	Lechfeld

2./NAG 6

Staffelkapitän	?/45	Oberleutnant Herward Braunegg
Gefechtsstand (HQ)		Oberleutnant Erich Weiss
TO (Technical)		Leutnant F-W Schlüter
Known bases:	8/44 to 11/9/44	Bayreuth-Bindlach
	11/9/44 to 12/44	Herzogenaurach
	12/44 to 27/2/45	Schwäbisch Hall
	27/2/45 to Mar 45	Hohne-Schleswig
	3/45 to 10/4/45	Burg
	10/4/45 to 12/4/45	Fassberg
	12/4/45 to 29/4/45	Lechfeld
	29/4/45 to 2/5/45	Kaltenkirchen
	2/5/45 to 8/5/45	Lechfeld

COLOUR PLATES

1
Me 262A-1a Wk-Nr. 170070 'White '12'/'E7+02' of the *Erprobungsstelle*, Rechlin, August 1944

Built at Leipheim, this aircraft was used to test the TSA 2D bombsight and *Wikingerschiff* bomb racks. The 'E7' in its code denotes Department E7 – Air-Dropped Weapons. Used for testing between August and December 1944, the jet was then sent to I./JG 7 in April 1945 and abandoned at the end of the war.

2
Me 262A-1a/U3 Wk-Nr. 170111 of *Kommando Braunegg/Kommando Panther*, Schwäbisch Hall, December 1945

Also built in Leipheim, this aircraft was flown by Oberleutnant Braunegg throughout the second half of 1944. Fitted with twin Rb 50/30 cameras and a single 30 mm MK 108 cannon in the forward nose compartment, the jet crash-landed on 1 January 1945 and suffered nosegear damage rated at five percent.

3
Me 262 V10 Wk-Nr. 130005/'VI+AE' of Messerschmitt AG, Lechfeld, January-July 1944

Built at Augsburg as the tenth prototype Me 262, this aircraft was used extensively throughout the first half of 1944 on bomb-dropping trials. The jet was flown during this period by Messerschmitt test pilots Gerd Lindner, Fritz Wendel and Oberleutnant Ernst Tesch. Depicted here fitted with *Wikingerschiff* racks for SC 500 bombs, the jet was later assigned to *Erprobungskommando* 262.

4
Me 262A-1a Wk-Nr. 130179/'Black F' of *Kommando Schenck*, Lechfeld, July 1944

Built at Schwäbisch Hall, this aircraft was one of the first Me 262s delivered to *Kommando Schenck* by Messerschmitt at Lechfeld in late June 1944. The jet was flown by Schenck and Batel, the latter reporting that Wk-Nr. 130179 was suffering from several build-related problems that adversely affected the functioning of a number of its systems. The aircraft was destroyed in a USAAF air raid on Lechfeld on 19 July 1944.

5
Me 262A-1a Wk-Nr. 170063(?)/'Black D' of *Kommando Schenck*, Lechfeld, July 1944

Also amongst the first batch of aircraft delivered to *Kommando Schenck*, this aircraft was finished in RLM 74 Grey Green and 75 Grey Violet on its fuselage and uppersurfaces, with RLM 76 Light Blue on its undersurfaces. Early *Kommando*

Schenck aircraft carried black identification letters outlined in white on the forward fuselage and nosewheel door. It is possible that this aircraft was Wk-Nr. 170063.

6
Me 262A Wk-Nr. 130303/'White V303' of Messerschmitt AG, Lechfeld, late 1944/early 1945
Built in Leipheim and designated the second V7 prototype following the loss of the first machine, this aircraft was used for a wide range of flight-testing including bomb dropping and bomb-release gear evaluation with concrete test bombs. The jet had *Wikingerschiff* bomb racks fitted for these trials.

7
Me 262A-2a Wk-Nr. 170096/'9K+BH' of 1./KG 51, Rheine, autumn 1944
Wk-Nr. 170096 was built in Leipheim and delivered to 1./KG 51 on 23 September 1944. The jet was camouflaged in a scribble pattern of greens' RLM 80 and 82, with RLM 76 pale blue on the undersides. The aircraft's nose cone and tail fin were marked in white, which was 1. *Staffel's* colour. 1./KG 51 reported numerous mechanical defects with this jet prior to it being badly damaged at Giebelstadt on 2 October 1944.

8
Me 262A-2a '9K+YH' of 1./KG 51, Rheine, autumn 1944
Typical of Me 262s operating with I./KG 51 in late 1944, this aircraft was finished in a scribble pattern of greens' RLM 80 and 82 with RLM 76 pale blue on its undersides. Again, its nose cone and tail fin are in 1. *Staffel* white.

9
Me 262A-2a Wk-Nr. 170064(?)/'9K+BK' of 2./KG 51, Rheine, October 1944
Believed to have been a Leipheim-built machine, Wk-Nr. 170064 was finished in a scribble pattern of RLM 80 and 82 greens, with RLM 76 pale blue undersides. 2. *Staffel's* red colour was applied to the individual aircraft code and nose cone. This aircraft was possibly flown by Leutnant Hans Heid.

10
Me 262A-a/U2 Wk-Nr. 110484/'White V484' of the *Erprobungsstelle*, Rechlin, early 1945
Constructed at Leipheim as a prototype *'Schnellstbomber'*, this aircraft was fitted with a Lotfe bombsight in an enlarged wooden nose and a glazed cone to accommodate a prone bomb-aimer. It undertook trials in late 1944/early 1945 using 250 kg bombs.

11
Me 262A-1a Wk-Nr. 111603 of Messerschmitt AG, Lechfeld, January 1945
Also built at Leipheim, this aircraft was used for bombing tests in January 1945. It is seen here in its ex-factory finish, without unit markings, as used for flying trials. Wk-Nr. 111603 was subsequently transferred to I./KG 51 at the beginning of February 1945.

12
Me 262A-1a/U3 Wk-Nr. 500259/'White 3' of 1./NAG 6, Eger or Lechfeld, March 1945
Built in Regensburg, this aircraft was converted into an A-1a/U3 at Eger and flight-tested by *Flugkapitän* Oeller on 19 March 1945. Transferred to 1./NAG 6 and flown by Unteroffizier Heinz Huxold, it appears to have been camouflaged in a blend of RLM 71 Dark Green and RLM 77 Dark Grey.

13
Me 262A-2a Wk-Nr. 110813 of Messerschmitt AG, Memmingen and Leipheim, January 1945
Built in December 1944 at Leipheim and used for bomb-dropping tests by Messerschmitt at Memmingen and Leipheim in January 1945, this aircraft was transferred to III./EJG 2 at Lechfeld for training purposes at the beginning of February. Subsequently, it may have been assigned to I./JG 7.

14
Me 262A-2a Wk-Nr. 111685/'White F' of 1./KG 51, Hopsten, March 1945
Built at Schwäbisch Hall, this aircraft displays typical late-war colours and white 1. *Staffel* markings. Delivered to 1./KG 51 at Hopsten on 15 March 1945, the jet was then transferred to Memmingen and, finally, to München-Riem, where it was assigned to JV 44. Wk-Nr. 111685 was found by Allied troops abandoned off an Autobahn at the end of war.

15
Me 262A-2a Wk-Nr. 110836/'Black L' of Hauptmann Rudolf Abrahamczik, 2./KG 51, Saaz, May 1945
Built at Leipheim and delivered to I./KG 51 in mid-March 1945, this aircraft was subsequently flown from Memmingen and then München-Riem, where it was assigned to JV 44. The jet was then transferred to Prague-Ruzyne, before heading to Saaz and back to München-Riem. It was flown from the latter airfield by Hauptmann Abrahamczik, *Kapitän* of 2. *Staffel*. After the war Wk-Nr. 110836 went to the USA for evaluation, after which it was eventually scrapped.

16
Me 262A-1a/U3 Wk-Nr. 500257/'White 2' of 1./NAG 1, Zerbst, April 1945
Built at Regensburg and known to be in service with NAG 1 by early April 1945, this aircraft had its individual number, '2', and nose marking (which also featured black and red bands) finished in 1. *Staffel* white. After a brief operational period of just two weeks, 'White 2' was destroyed by retreating Luftwaffe personnel at Bernburg on 12 April 1945.

17
Me 262A-2a Wk-Nr. 500200/'Black X' of Leutnant Hans-Robert Fröhlich, 2./KG 51, Fassberg, May 1945

Built at Regensburg, 'Black X' was finished in a blend of RLM 81 Brown Violet and 82 Olive Green, with RLM 76 Light Blue undersides. The nose cone and tailfin tip were painted red to denote the jet's assignment to 2. *Staffel*. Fröhlich flew this aircraft from Saaz into British capitvity at Fassberg on 8 May 1945.

18
Me 262A-1a/U3 Wk-Nr. 500098/'27' of 1./NAG 6, Lechfeld, May 1945

Built in Regensburg, this aircraft was converted into an A-1a/U3 at Eger and test-flown in early February 1945, before being delivered to NAG 6. Captured at Lechfeld, '27' was taken over by the USAAF's 54th Air Disarmament Squadron and flown to France, from where it was shipped to the USA. The jet was written off in a crash there in August 1945.

19
Me 262A-1a/U3 Wk-Nr. 500453/'25' of 1./NAG 6, Lechfeld, May 1945

Also constructed in Regensburg, this aircraft was converted into an A-1a/U3 at Eger and test-flown on 14 March 1945 by Messerschmitt test pilot Otto Kaiser. It was then delivered to 1./NAG 6 and ultimately captured at Lechfeld. The jet's camouflage consists of possible overspraying of RLM 82 and RLM 77 over a previous solid RLM 80/82 scheme.

20
Me 262A-1a/U3 '26' probably of 1./NAG 6, Lechfeld, May 1945

'26' was finished in what appears to be a scribble pattern of RLM 82 Olive Green and 02 Grey over a base colour of RLM 77 Dark Grey. This aircraft was amongst the handful of Me 262A-1a/U3s shipped to America after the war, where it undertook speed trials with the USAAF.

21
Me 262A-1a/U3 Wk-Nr. 500853/'29' probably of 1./NAG 6, Lechfeld, May 1945

Built at Obertraubling, this aircraft was found abandoned by Allied forces at Lechfeld. Its scribble pattern camouflage was probably formed of RLM 81 and 82 over RLM 77.

22
Me 262A-1a/U3 '30' probably of 1./NAG 6, Lechfeld, May 1945

Also captured intact at Lechfeld, this aircraft probably served with NAG 6. It was shipped to the USA under the 'management' of the 54th Air Disarmament Squadron post-VE-Day. The jet was subsequently passed on to the US Navy, but the Me 262 crashed on its first test flight on 7 November 1945 and was written off.

23
Me 262A-1a/U3 Wk-Nr. 500539/'33' probably of 1./NAG 6, Lechfeld, May 1945

Built in Regensburg, this aircraft boasts the widely adopted scribble-pattern camouflage that was used by NAG 6 on its Me 262s. The jet was tested by *Flugkapitän* Oeller at Eger on 16 March 1945, before being flown to Lechfeld. It was found here by the Allies following the German surrender.

24
Me 262A-1a/U3 '34' possibly of NAG 6 or I./KG 51, München-Riem, May 1945

The U3 reconnaissance nose of this aircraft has been replaced with a standard A-1a fighter nose, finished in Ikarol 201 Green. The outline of the camera blister fitment can still be seen just forward of the '34'. The aircraft has a heavy scribble of RLM 82 over RLM 77 – note also its replacement engine intake rings. Found abandoned at Riem, this jet could have been an aircraft that was taken over by KG 51 following its re-conversion to A-1a specification at Lechfeld and then transferred to Riem.

Back Cover
Me 262B-1a Wk-Nr. 110639/'35' possibly of 2./NAG 6, Schleswig, May 1945

Built in Leipheim, this aircraft is believed to have been converted into a two-seat B-1a trainer by Blohm und Voss in March 1945 – it was recorded as being coded 'BV 35' at this time. However, the jet's capture at the northern airfield of Schleswig (used by 2./NAG 6 in late March) and the styling of the aircraft numbers on the previously illustrated Me 262s from NAG 6 tends to suggest that this was one of the very few (only?) trainers assigned to the *Gruppe*. Wk-Nr. 110639 was also shipped to the USA post-war.

BIBLIOGRAPHY

UNPUBLISHED MATERIAL

UK NATIONAL ARCHIVES, KEW

AIR8/786 *Enemy Jet-Propelled Aircraft*, ID3/990(C), November 1944 to February 1945

AIR22/81 *Air Ministry Weekly Intelligence Summaries* 266-286, October 1944 to February 1945

AIR20/7708 *The Western Front 1-14 February 1945 – Daily situation reports issued by OKL Operatons Staff Ia*, AHB6 Translation No VII/130, April 1954

AIR20/7708 *The Western Front 15-28 February 1945 – Daily situation reports issued by OKL Operatons Staff Ia*, AHB6 Translation No VII/131, April 1954

AIR20/7709 AHB.6 Translation No VII/137 *Fighter Staff Conferences 1944*, June 1954

AIR25/698 *No 83 (Composite) Group Operations Record Book, Appendices,* April 1943 to February 1946

AIR26/187 *No 127 Airfield (RCAF), Operations Record Book*, July 1943 to July 1945

AIR29/105 *RAF Regiment Squadrons*, September 1941 to April 1946

AIR40/2046 *Recent Activities of I. & II./KG 51*, Wg Cdr Hurst, undated

AIR40/2377 *HQ 2nd TAF Signal Intelligence Survey of GAF Activity – month of February 1945*, March 1945

DEFE3/504/565/566/567/568/569/571/572/601 Ultra Decrypt and HW5/685 *Reports of German Army and Air Force High Grade Machine Decrypts*, 1-2 April 1945/686, 3-4 April 1945/688 and 7-8 April 1945

WO171/1087 *100 Bde, Anti-Aircraft Brigades*, January-December 1944

MISCELLANEOUS

Major Schenck, *Kommodore* KG 51, Br.B.Nr. Ia 613/44, 29/10/44

Kampfgeschwader 51 – *Kommodore*, B.Nr. 663/44: *Einsatzbefehl für I./KG 51*, 9/12/44

'The Me 262 as a Combat Aircraft', ADI(K) Report No 323/1945, 4 June 1945

'GAF Jet-Propelled Aircraft', HQ AAF Intelligence Report No 45-102, 10 February 1945, Office of the Assistant Chief of Air Staff, Intelligence, Washington, D.C.

Luftwaffenkommando West and AOC Norway and Italy: Morning and Evening Situation Reports – February-April 1945

'Zugang aus Industrie' Stand 31/3/45 and 10/4/45 (prepared for OKL *Führungsstab*)

PUBLISHED ARTICLES

BEALE, NICK, *I./NAG 1 and the Me 262: January-April 1945* at www.ghostbombers.com

BEALE, NICK, *Einsatzkommando KG 51: 24-31 August 1944* at www.ghostbombers.com

GRIEHL, MANFRED, *Blitzbomber*, *Flugzeug* 6/90

HAEFNER, HEINRICH, *Die letzten Einsätze der deutschen Luftwaffe mit der Messerschmitt Me 262 vom 1. Januar-8 Mai 1945*, Luftwaffen-Revue 2/98

JACK, UWE W, *Strahlbomber – Einsatz der Me 262 beim KG 51*, *Berliner Flug*, January 1986

JACK, UWE W, *Strahlbomber – Zweiter Teil*, *Berliner Flug*, July 1986

JACK, UWE W, *Strahlbomber* (*Leserpost*), *Berliner Flug*, January 1987

SCHMOLL, PETER, *Me 262 beim KG 51* – letter in *Flugzeug*, 2/91

Various unit data at www.ww2.dk

SELECTED BOOKS

BEALE, NICK, *Kampfflieger Volume Four, Summer 1943-May 1945*, Classic Publications, Hersham, 2005

BOEHME, MANFRED, *Strahlaufklärer Messerschmitt Me 262 – Die Geschichte der Nahaufklärungsgruppe 6*, VDM Heinz Nickel, Zweibrücken, 2000

BROWN D E, JANDA A, PORUBA T and VLADAR J, *Luftwaffe over Czech Territory – Messerschmitt Me 262s of KG & KG(J) units*, JaPo, Hradec Králové, 2010

BRÜTTING, GEORG, *Das waren die deutschen Kampfflieger Asse 1939-1945*, Motorbuch Verlag, Stuttgart, 1975

O'CONNELL, DAN, *Messerschmitt Me 262 – The Production Log 1941-1945*, Classic Publications, Hersham, 2005

DIERICH, WOLFGANG, *Kampfgeschwader 'Edelweiss' – The History of a German Bomber Unit 1939-1945*, Ian Allan, Shepperton, 1975

ELLIS, MAJ L F, with WARHURST, LT COL A E, *History of the Second World War – Victory in the West: Volume II The Defeat of Germany*, HMSO, London, 1968

ELSTOB, PETER, *Battle of the Reichswald*, Macdonald & Co, London, 1971

FARRAR-HOCKLEY, ANTHONY, *Airborne Carpet – Operation Market Garden*, Macdonald & Co, London, 1969

HORN, JAN, *Das Flurschaden-Geschwader – Die Chronik des Kampfgeschwaders 51 "Edelweiß" zwischen dem 1. Januar 1944 bis Kriegsende*, Jan Horn, Dresden, 2010

KAISER, JOCHEN, *Die Ritterkreuzträger der Kampfflieger – Band 1*, Luftfahrtverlag Start, Bad Zwischenhahn, 2010

KERSHAW, ROBERT J, *'It never snows in September': The German View of Market Garden and the Battle of Arnhem, September 1944*, The Crowood Press, Marlborough, 1990

NEILLANDS, ROBIN, *The Battle for the Rhine 1944 – Arnhem and the Ardennes: the Campaign in Europe*, Weidenfeld & Nicolson, London, 2005

PARKER, DANNY S, *To Win the Winter Sky – Air War over the Ardennes 1944-1945*, Greenhill Books, London, 1994

SCHMOLL, PETER, *Nest of Eagles – Messerschmitt Production and Flight-Testing at Regensburg 1936-1945*, Classic Publications, Hersham, 2009

SHORES, CHRISTOPHER and THOMAS, CHRIS, *2nd Tactical Air Force Volume Two: Breakout to Bodenplatte – July 1944 to January 1945*, Classic Publications, Hersham, 2005

SCHRAMM, PERCY E (Hrsg), *Kriegstagbuch des Oberkommandos der Wehrmacht 1944-1945 Teilband II*, Bernard & Graefe Verlag, München, 1982

SMITH, J RICHARD and CREEK, EDDIE J, *Me 262 Volume One*, Classic Publications, Burgess Hill, 1997

SMITH, J RICHARD and CREEK, EDDIE J, *Me 262 Volume Two*, Classic Publications, Burgess Hill, 1998

SMITH, J RICHARD and CREEK, EDDIE J, *Me 262 Volume Three*, Classic Publications, Crowborough, 2000

SMITH, J RICHARD and CREEK, EDDIE J, *Me 262 Volume Four*, Classic Publications, Crowborough, 2000

STAPFER, HANS-HEIRI, *Me 262 in Action*, Squadron Signal Publications, Carrollton, 2008

TAGHON, PETER, *Die Geschichte des Lehrgeschwaders 1 – Band 2 1942-1945*, VDM Heinz Nickel, Zweibrücken, 2004

URBANKE, AXEL, *Green Hearts – First in Combat with the Dora 9 – The Men of III./JG 54 and JG 26 unite in defense of their homeland 1944-1945*, Eagle Editions, Hamilton, 1998

WADMAN, DAVID, BRADLEY, JOHN and KETLEY, BARRY, *Aufklärer – Luftwaffe Reconnaissance Aircraft & Units 1935-1945*, Hikoki Publications, Aldershot 1997

WADMAN, DAVID, *Aufklärer – Luftwaffe Reconnaissance Aircraft and Units 1942-1945, Volume Two*, Classic Publications, Hersham, 2007

WIESINGER, GUNTER and SCHROEDER, WALTER, *Die Osterreichischen Ritterkreuzträger in der Luftwaffe 1939-45*, H Weishaupt Verlag, Graz, 1986

ZENG IV, DE, HENRY L and STANKEY, DOUGLAS G, *Bomber Units of the Luftwaffe – A Reference Source, Volume 1*, Midland Publishing, Hinckley, 2007

INDEX

References to illustrations are shown in **bold**. Plates are shown with page and caption locators in brackets.

Abrahamczik, Hptm Rudolf **4**, **13**, **22**, 35, **36**, 36–37, **37**, 38, 39, **40**, 41, 43, 44, **54**, 61, 63, 64, **15**(72, 92), **86**, 87, 88
Albersmeyer, Oblt Ludwig **13**, **36**, **42**
Arado Ar 234: **12**

Batel, Lt Wilhelm **16**, 16, 26–27, 35, 37, 38, **40**, 46, 55, 56, 58, 78, 85, 87, 88, 91
Baur, Karl **87**
Below, ObstLt Nicolaus von 10
Bentrott, Uffz Walter 16–17
Boyle, Flt Lt Jack 46
Braunegg, Hptm Herward 15, **49**, 49, 50, **57**, 58, 80, **81**, 84, 91
British Army: XXX Corps 23, 26, 27, 28, 31, 62; 1st Airborne Division 26, 27; 21st Army Group 23; Royal Engineers **34**; Second Army 26, 62
Brücker, Maj Heinrich 39–40, 59, 60, 86
Bruhn, Ofw Helmut **16**, **42**, 87
Buttmann, Hptm Hans-Christoph 26–27, 31–33, **34**

cameras, Zeiss 48, **49**, **57**, **67**
Canadian Air Force, Royal: No 127 Wing 30, 35; No 401 Sqn 31–33; No 403 Sqn 46; No 411 Sqn 46; No 416 Sqn 27, 29; No 439 Sqn 63; No 441 Sqn 27
Capitain, Fw Karl-Albrecht 15, **16**, 39, 41, 42, 44, **81**, 82, 85
Cole, Plt Off Bob 34, 40
Collier, Sqn Ldr James 46
Cowan, Lt Oliven C **66**, 66
Csurusky, Hptm Georg **13**, 15, **16**, **22**, 33, 35, 41, **42**, 42, 43, **54**

INDEX

Dennis, Flt Lt R V 58

Edwards, Lt Harry L 43
Engelhart, Oblt 49, 50, 60
Engels, Oblt Erich 79
Esche, Lt Fritz 41, 42, 44, 81

Färber, Uffz Alfred 56
Fraser, Flg Off Hugh 63
Fröhlich, Lt Hans-Robert 39, **17**(73, 93), 87, **88**, **89**

Galland, Genlt Adolf 11, **38**, 79, 86, 87
Garland, Flt Lt J W 42
German Army: 5. *Panzer Armee* 47; 6. *Panzer Armee* 44, 45
Golde, Uffz Martin 40, 63, 76
Göring, *Reichsmarschall* Hermann 8–9, **9**, 10, 11–12, 35, 52, 62, 64–65, 77
Grundmann, Hptm Hans-Joachim 37, 42, 44, 45, 46, 84, 85–86
Gutzmer, Hptm Dr Hans 40–41, 43, 44, 45, 76–77

Haeffner, Oblt Heinrich 36–38, 39, **40**, 40, 44, 47, 54, 55, 56, 58–59, 61, 63–64, 81, 82, 84, 85, 87, 88, **89**, 89
Hallensleben, ObstLt Rudolf von 27, **59**, 59, 85
Heid, Lt Hans 40, 44, **53**, 58, 59, 81
Helbig, Obst Joachim 24, 27
Hitler, Adolf 6, 7, 8, **9**, 9, 10, 11, **12**, 12, 19, 23, 25, 38, 44, 83
Hofmann, Willie 87
Hoiß, Inspektor Hans 47
Hovestadt, Oblt Harald **47**, **78**, 78
Huxold, Uffz Heinz **65**, 65, 92

Kaiser, Ofw Erich **16**, 33, **34**, **36**, 39, **42**, **43**, 43, **54**, 54–55
Kammhuber, Genmaj Josef 79, 82, 84
Keck, Oblt Georg **58**, 58
Kettenkrad semi-tracked tractor **28**, **39**, **58**, 67
Knobloch, Heinz 13
Knoll, Oblt Wilhelm 56, 65
Konantz, Lt Walter J 56

Lamle, Oblt Hans-Georg 46
Lange, Lt Hubert 58, 59, 61, 82
Lauer, Ofw Hieronymous 20, 21–22, 23, 25, 31, 85
Lucht, *Generalingenieur* Roluf **9**
Luftwaffe 6
 III./EJG 2: **51**, **58**, **66**, **67**, 83
 Erprobungskommando 262: 15;
   Erprobungsschwarm des Generals der Schlachtflieger 39–40, 59–60;
   Erprobungsstelle **1**(68, 91), **10**(71, 92)
 Gefechtsverband: Hallensleben 27, 28, 33; *Helbig* 24; *Hogeback* 86–88; *Kowalewski* 64–65, 77
 JG 27: 38
 V./KG 2: **13**
 KG 51: 15–16, 28, 29, 33, 39, 41, 58, **62**, 76, 79–80, 82, 83, 85, 86, 87; I./KG 51: **4**, 13, **14**, 16, 17, 19, 20, 27, 28–30, 34, 35, 39, 40, 41–42, 44–45, 52–54, **53**, 55–56, 59, 60–61, 62, **64**, 64–66, 67, **24**(75, 93), **77**, 77, 81, 82, 84, 85, 86; II./KG 51: **4**, 20, 27, 37, 38–39, 41, 43, 44, 46, 47, 59, 61, 62, 64–65, 76, 77, 78, 82, 83, 84, 85–86; III./KG 51: 39; IV./KG 51: 41; 1./KG 51: **24**, **28**, **32**, 35, **45**, **53**, **7**, **8**(70, 92), **14**(72, 92), **78**; 2./KG 51: **4**, 35, 36–37, 38, 39, 40, **41**, **55**, **9**(70, 92), **15**(72, 92), **17**(73, 93), **86**, **89**; 3./KG 51: 17, 18, 31, 33, 35, 37, 43; 4./KG 51: 43; 5./KG 51: 43, 61; 6./KG 51: 42, 46, 78; *Einsatzkommando* I./KG 51: 18, 21, 24, 27, 28, 29–30, 33, 34–35; *Stab*/KG 51: 16, 19, 20, 37, 41, 43
 KG 76: 62, 63, 64–65, 67; III./KG 76: 76, 77
 Kommando: Braunegg (later *Panther*) **49**, 49–51, **57**, 58, 59, **2**(68, 91); *Schenck* (3./KG 51 *Einsatzkommando*) 14, 15, **17**, 18, 19–21, **20**, **21**, 22, 23–25, 26, 27, 31, 35, **4**(69, 91), **5**(69, 91–92); *Sperling* 24
 NAG 1: 56–58, 67, 84–85; 1./NAG 1: **16**(73, 92), **78**, **83**, 83
 NAG 6: 50–51, 60, 61–62, **63**, 65, 66, **24**(75, 93), 78–79, **80**, 81, 83, 85, 87; 1./NAG 6: 65, **12**(71, 92), **18**(73, 93), **19–21**(74, 93), **22**, **23**(75, 93), 78; 2./NAG 6 (formerly *Kommando Panther*) 62, 67, 76, 78, 84, **93**; *Stab*/NAG 6: 78

Maser, Lt Albert **40**
McLeod, Flt Lt F L 58
Messerschmitt, Prof. Willi 6, 8–10, **9**, 12
Messerschmitt Me 262: **21**, **45**, **52**;
 Aufklärer (reconnaissance) proposals 48; 'Black 0' **89**; bomb containers **20**, **21**; bomb racks 13, **14**, 16, **17**, **60**, **64**; bombing missions 38; ground-attack role 59–60; nose **32**; performance figures 35–36; *Schnellbomber* proposals **7**, 7, **8**; sight, *Revi* reflector 13–14, 18, 21, 38; 'White 6' **77**
 Me 262 S1 10–11; Me 262 S3 11; Me 262 S7 10
 Me 262 V2 6–7; Me 262 V3 6; Me 262 V6 9; Me 262 V7 10; Me 262 V8 **16**; Me 262 V10 **3**(68, 91)
 Me 262A **6**(69, 92)
 Me 262A-1a 7; Wk-Nr. 110613 **4**; Wk-Nr. 111603 **60**, **64**, **11**(71, 92); Wk-Nr. 130179 **17**, 18, **4**(69, 91); Wk-Nr. 170063(?) **20**, **5**(69, 91–92); Wk-Nr. 170070 **1**(68, 91); Wk-Nr. 170106 **4**; Wk-Nr. 170111 **57**, **2**(68, 91)
 Me 262A-1a/U3 *Behelfsaufklärer* 48–49, 51, 81; '26' **20**(74, 93); '30' **22**(75, 93); '34' **24**(75, 93); 'Red 27' **87**; 'White 2' **83**; 'White 3' **51**; Wk-Nr. 170006 50; Wk-Nr. 500098 **18**(73, 93); Wk-Nr. 500257 **16**(73, 92); Wk-Nr. 500259 **58**, **66**, **67**, **12**(71, 92); Wk-Nr. 500453 **19**(74, 93); Wk-Nr. 500539 **23**(75, 93); Wk-Nr. 500853 **21**(74, 93)
 Me 262A-2a 14, 18–19, **55**; armament 13–14; equipment 16; '9K+YH' **14**, **24**, **8**(70, 92); tactics 29, **62**; Wk-Nr. 110813 **10**, **13**(72, 92); Wk-Nr. 110836 **15**(72, 92); **86**; Wk-Nr. 111685 **14**(72, 92); Wk-Nr. 170064(?) **39**, **9**(70, 92); Wk-Nr. 170096 **28**, **7**(70, 92), **78**; Wk-Nr. 170229 **41**; Wk-Nr. 500200 **17**(73, 93), **89**
 Me 262A-5a 48
 Me 262A-a/U2 **10**(71, 92)

Me 262B-1a **93**
Messerschmitt Me 410: **13**, 13
Meyer, Fw Hans 39, 40, 46–47
Milch, GFM Erhard 8, 10, 11, 12
Montgomery, FM Bernard 26

Nijmegen bridge 27, **29**, 29, 31

Oldenstädt, Ofw Fritz **83**, 83, 89
operations: *Bodenplatte* 52–55, **53**; *Goodwood* 17; *Market Garden* 26–28

Peltz, Genmaj Dietrich 19, 42, 52, 88
Piehl, Lt Kurt **66**, 66
Prehl, Ofw Siegfried **42**

Riese, Unterarzt Dr Wolfgang **80**, 81
Ritter-Rittershain, Oblt Oswald von 36–37, 39, **40**, 40, 56
Rösch, Hptm Rudolf 39, **40**, 40, **78**
Royal Air Force squadrons: No 3: 34, 40; No 56: 58; No 80: 42; No 132: 28; No 332: 56
Rundstedt, GFM Gerd von 23

Sanio, Offz Horst 39, 40, **41**
Saur, *Hauptdienstleiter* Karl-Otto 11, **12**, 12, 16
Schenck, ObstLt Wolfgang 'Bombo' 14–15, **15**, 23, 35–36, 45, 46, 52–53, 59
Schlüter, Oblt F W 49, 50, **80**, 81
Schmidt, Fw Werner **42**, 42
Schubert, Lt Herbert 60, **61**, **80**, 81
Schultze, Maj Friedrich Heinz 50, **58**, 58, 84, 89
Shaver, Flt Lt Lyall C 63
Smith, Sqn Ldr Rod 31–33, **33**
Speer, Albert 10, 11, 12
Stephan, Oblt Gustav 37, 56, 79
Streit, Ofw Otto 38, 40
Strothmann, Oblt Heinz 39, **56**, 56, 87, 88
Supermarine Spitfire **30**

Tetzner, Lt Hellmut **60**, 60, 80, 88–89
Threlkeld, Lt Thomas N 66
Trenke, Fw Johann 'Hans' 47, 61

Unrau, Maj Heinz **13**, 13, **19**, **22**, 22, 35, **36**, **37**, **38**, **42**, **47**, **54**, 54, **78**, 84
US Army: VII Corps 77; 82nd Airborne Division 26, 27, 31, 60; 101st Airborne Division 26; First Army 23, 26, 28, 34, 44, 66, 77; Ninth Army 44, 66, 76; Third Army 23
US Army Air Forces: 54th Air Disarmament Sqn **87**, 93; 55th FG 56; 91st BG 42; 324th FG 56; 352nd FG 43; 365th FG **66**, 66, 67; 366th, 373rd & 405th FGs 67; Eighth Air Force 79, 84; and Me 262 threat **29**, **62**; Ninth Air Force 45

Valet, Oblt Hans-Joachim 41, **42**, 42
Vlasov Army 88

Wacht-am-Rhein counter-offensive **4**, 44–47, 51, 52
weapons: bombs **4**, **10**, **21**, **60**, **64**; cannon 7
Weiss, Oblt Erich 50, **80**, 81
Wendel, Fritz 6, 18–19, **19**, 21–22, 25, 26, 91
Wieczorek, Ofw Hermann **4**, 43, 44, 46–47, 56, 63, 64
Winkel, Hptm Eberhard 13, 17, 18, 27, 35, **36**, 36, **37**, **54**, 79